George Giusti
The Idea Is the
Heart of the Matter

BY NED DREW

BRENDA MCMANUS

AND PAUL STERNBERGER

GEORGE

GIUSTI

George Giusti
**The Idea Is the
Heart of the Matter**

BY NED DREW

BRENDA MCMANUS

AND PAUL STERNBERGER

CARY GRAPHIC DESIGN
ARCHIVE
CHAPBOOK SERIES: SIX

RIT PRESS
2016

George Giusti
The Idea Is the
Heart of the Matter

BY NED DREW

BRENDA MCMANUS

AND PAUL STERNBERGER

CARY GRAPHIC DESIGN
ARCHIVES
CHAPBOOK SERIES: SIX

RIT PRESS

90 Lomb Memorial Drive
Rochester, New York 14623-5604
http://ritpress.rit.edu

Front and back cover: *Portrait of Giusti,* 1949,
Photograph by Jeff Moses

ISBN 978-1-939125-30-9 Printed in USA

Library of Congress Cataloging-in-Publication Data

Names	Drew, Ned, author.	McManus, Brenda, 1973– author.	Sternberger, Paul Spencer, 1966– author.
Title	George Giusti: the idea is the heart of the matter / Ned Drew, Brenda McManus, Paul Sternberger.
Description	Rochester, New York: RIT Cary Graphic Arts Press, 2016.
Identifiers	LCCN 2016020483 (print)	LCCN 2016020899 (ebook)	ISBN 9781939125309 (pbk.: alk. paper)	ISBN 9781939125316 (e-book)
Subjects	LCSH: Giusti, George, 1908–1991– Criticism and interpretation.
Classification	LCC NC999.4.G53 D74 2016 (print)	LCC NC999.4.G53 (ebook)	DDC 741.092–dc23	LC record available at https://lccn.loc.gov/2016020483

George Giusti

1 George Giusti, "Some of My Ideas,"
included with a letter and questionnaire
about *Fortune* sent to Phil Beard,
December 22, 1984, 3.
George Giusti Collection,
Cary Graphic Arts Collection at
The Wallace Center,
Rochester Institute of Technology.

I believe that every true artist is a discoverer, forever seeking new horizons to explore. His is a continual search for clues that help him envision the world of tomorrow.

He looks upon excepted [sic] forms and conventions not as immutable laws, but as forerunners of the new concepts and solutions.

He is a free man, and is not ruled by notions of what must be and what must not be....

The true artist delves deeply into his own fantasies. But he is no idle dreamer; his feet are on firm ground. The unconscious is a bottomless reservoir from which he draws the raw material for his creativity. With his conscious mind he takes the nebulous and translates it into logical and useful concepts. Thus he turns dreams into reality and relates them to the present. It is impossible to be creative without this interchange between fantasy and the real.

To dream is natural, but it takes work, and more work, to mold vague ideas into an art and a reality that is far above and beyond the easy alternatives of the past or present.[1]

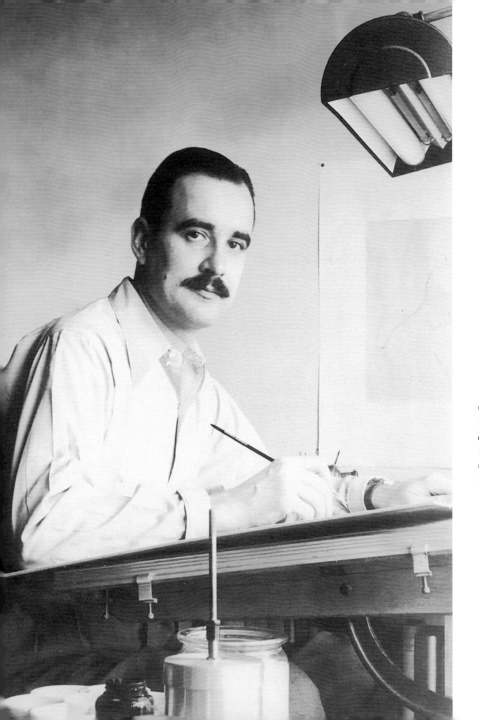

Giusti at work in his
Bronx apartment
c. 1943
Photograph from the
Collection of
Robert Giusti

George Giusti
The Idea Is the Heart of the Matter

BY NED DREW, BRENDA MCMANUS AND PAUL STERNBERGER

2 Quoted in Alison Bert
"Our George Giusti," *Guitar Review*
(Winter 1990): 24.

No Idle Dreamer: The Foundations of Disciplined Design

Remembering his father in 1990, Robert Giusti concluded, "Basically, he was an aesthete. He spoke with an aesthete's vocabulary and he lived an aesthete's life. He believed that things should look good and be well made, and that they should be of the highest quality and perfect. Perfection was the key word with my father. No matter what you did–whether it was tying your shoelace or creating a piece of sculpture, it was perfection that he sought."[2] Indeed, George Giusti (1908–1990) was a perfectionist who held himself to the highest standards of technique, concept, and innovation. Giusti's mental dexterity, demanding principles, and creative resolve were rooted in a fine art tradition, but he was determined to be neither stymied nor pigeonholed by convention. He was dedicated to fine craft, but unimpressed by craft alone; he was pragmatic about the functional demands on design, but he dismissed limiting distinctions between art and design; and he understood his practice of design as ever transforming, but always a continuum. In a professional career that spanned more than half a century, Giusti continuously evolved and broadened as a designer, creating interconnected bodies of work in graphic design, sculpture, and architecture. But as diverse as his pursuits would become, he never strayed from his steadfast dedication to fine technique placed in the service of rigorously considered concepts, a delicate dance of innovative experimentation balanced with proven principles of tradition.

3 Authors' interview with Robert Giusti, August 27, 2014.

4 George Giusti, *Drawing Figures* (New York and London: The Studio Publications, Inc., 1944), 7.

5 Georgine Oeri, "George Giusti, Graphic Artist," *Graphis* 5, no. 26 (1949): 148; Walter H. Allner, *Posters: Fifty Artists and Designers Analyze Their Approach, Their Methods, and Their Solutions to Poster Design and Poster Advertising* (New York: Reinhold Publishing Company, 1952), 46. His attendance in technical school is also mentioned in Pauline Engel, "George Giusti Joins Our Guiding Faculty," *Famous Artists Magazine* 9, no. 2 (Winter 1950): n.p.

6 Robert Giusti recalls being told that among his father's teachers at Brera were painter Giorgio Morandi and sculptor Marino Marini, though Marini did not receive a professorship at Brera until 1940. Authors' interview with Robert Giusti, August 27, 2014.

7 Giusti, *Drawing Figures*, 10.

George Giusti was born in 1908 of a Swiss father, Emilio Wurmli, and an Italian mother, Edmeda Giusti, who had settled in Milan.[3] The young Giusti gravitated toward graphic expression, and visualization of narrative seemed to come early to him—he recalled projects when he was just four years old in which he and his sister created piles of drawings elaborately illustrating the adventures of their invented character "Amabile." His dedication to drawing continued into his teens, when he avidly copied pictures "of every type, without discrimination."[4] At fifteen, after taking his initial studies at Milan's Scuola Tecnica (perhaps reflecting a boyhood ambition to be an engineer), Giusti started his art education in earnest after enrolling in the Accademia di Belle Arti di Brera in Milan.[5] Highly competitive and extremely rigorous, the training he received there was traditional and broadly focused, including figure drawing, anatomy, perspective, architecture, ornamental drawing, history of art and costume, and sculpture.[6]

The primacy of technique and process in a variety of media at the Brera Academy solidified a foundation of disciplined, multifaceted craft upon which Giusti would build his career as a designer. Giusti recalled intense prolonged work as a student on single drawings in which he rendered, erased, and reworked an image on a single piece of paper for months at a time. "Such a procedure," recounted Giusti, "naturally resulted in our paper becoming very dirty and rough and difficult to draw on at all, but our protests were silenced with the reprimand that we must master our craft no matter how inferior the materials we used, our skill would insure good work."[7]

George Giusti
untitled painting
c. 1920s
Collection of Robert Giusti

Giusti's education at Brera seems to have served him well as
his professional career evolved–the intensity of those exercises
guided him throughout his career and helped formulate
his exacting approach to problem solving and form giving.
The meticulous precision of his drawings, the deliberate nature
of his sketches, and his ability to embrace a variety of media
and styles with confidence and innovativeness all seem rooted
in skills he honed in his foundational studies.

8 Daniel Forte and Shinichiro Tora,
   "'90 The Art Directors Club Hall of Fame,"
   Idea 225 (1991): 45; "Art Directors Club
   Hall of Fame: George Giusti," program for
   Induction Ceremony, October 23, 1979: 128;
   Authors' interview with Robert Giusti,
   August 27, 2014. It was at this time that
   Giusti probably worked with pioneering
   Italian poster artist and fellow Brera
   graduate Giuseppe Cappadonia, who,
   in 1963, called Giusti his "first unforgettable
   disciple." Inscription to Giusti in Italian,
   dated January 1963.
   Collection of Robert Giusti.

9 For Swiss work with a "Giusti" signature,
   see "Design Dossier: Giusti,"
   Art and Industry, (September 1939), 144–7

10 Fridolf Johnson, "George Giusti,
    Graphic Designer," *American Artist* 28,
    no. 10 (December 1, 1964): 48, 50.

Following his graduation from the Brera Academy of Fine Arts, Giusti intended to pursue a career as a painter, but he was drawn to the world of advertising and had a very active career for three years as a graphic designer for an advertising agency in Milan before moving to Switzerland.[8] Giusti became an art director in Lugano, Switzerland, and then had his own studio in Zurich for seven years. It is not clear when or why Giusti began using his mother's surname, but he did not wait to adopt her name until after coming to America, as some sources have suggested—examples of his Swiss work carried a "Giusti" signature, and a stamp on a small leather box in the Robert Giusti collection read "GIORGIO GIUSTI, GRAPHIKER-UND REKLAMEBERATER" (Graphics and Publicity Expert), suggesting he was going by Giusti in Zurich.[9] It was in Switzerland that Giusti, according to author and art director Fridolf Johnson, developed the valuable attribute of "a well articulated thinking cap." Johnson went on to describe the characteristics of Swiss graphic design that Giusti had internalized: "The work of the graphic artists of Switzerland is like the bracing air of that mountainous country—transparent, because the idea behind each design is transmitted to the comprehension; clean, because all foggy, nebulous thinking has been filtered out. The problem and the solution have been made crystal clear, and they are stated in terms that are aesthetically pleasing."[10] Indeed, in these early years, Giusti seems to have developed the ability to balance fine technique and narrative illustration with more abstract, conceptual content, all put into the service of the carefully considered communication of an idea. In his design for a promotional folder for the Swiss department store Globus, Giusti built his composition around a close-up photograph he made of hands threading a needle.

Men's Fashion Folder
for Globus, Zurich, 1938.
Illustrated in
"George Giusti," *AD* 7,
no. 4 (April–May 1941): 5.

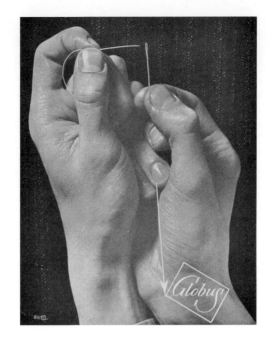

11 Ernest Watson, "Giusti,"
American Artist 74 (April 1, 1943): 16.
In the 1940s, Giusti was said to do his own
photography when he incorporated the
medium into his designs. In the caption for
a Globus pamphlet using the same image,
the photograph is credited to Giusti.
"Design Dossier: Giusti," 144.

The tension of the physical and mental exactitude required
for the act served as a simple, clear reference to the precision
in detail and craftsmanship of the clothing line as a whole.
The viewer's eye was drawn into the composition on the top
left and immediately became engaged in the tension and focus
of the delicate act of thread being guided into the eye of the
needle. Then the eye moved down the needle through the
hands into the arrow delicately pushing onto the corner of
the logo, once again reinforcing the precision and detail.
By 1939, Giusti was reported as touting "the idea" as "the
main feature of all designs for advertising; it is the keystone
on which rests the entire foundation. The graphic solution,
certainly, is not without consequence, but it must serve
the idea and not its own purposes."[11]

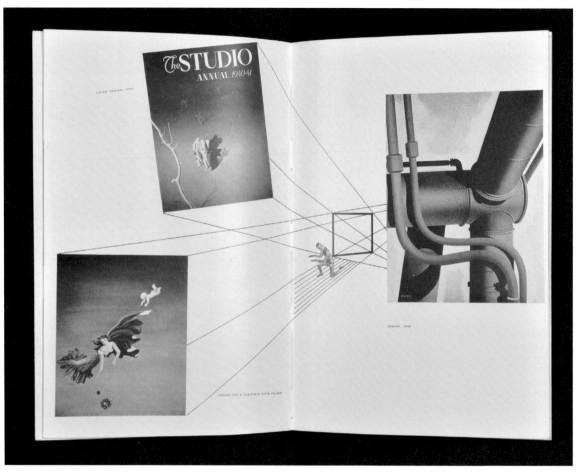

Giusti, layout for a feature article
on his design.
"George Giusti," *AD* 7, no. 4
(April–May 1941): 8–9.

12 "Design Dossier: Giusti," 144–7.
Giusti continued working for some of
his European clients after immigrating
to the United States.

Very little of Giusti's early European work has survived, but illustrations of some of Giusti's projects from the 1930s give a sense of the range of his European work: pamphlets and price lists for Globus; the program for the first Tour de Suisse bicycling race in 1933; labels for cheese; posters for the wool and fruit industries. As a whole, these early examples revealed elements that would inform his later work, including a refined sense of typography, an integration of bold photography with type and versatility in draftsmanship.[12] A 1941 feature article on Giusti's work in the design journal *AD* revealed not just the nature of some of his Swiss and early American work illustrated, but also a sense of his design aesthetic in the layout of the article, which Giusti himself designed for the journal. He mixed straightforward reproductions of his work with photographic fragments, geometric and linear symbols, and playfully understated angled lines of type to create a dynamic balance of text and image. Graphic elements were included, such as lines that added structure while acting as anchors for the images. Rather than merely illustrating examples of his work on the page, Giusti achieved a sense of perspective in a carefully considered composition, making the white space feel voluminous and vast, creating a greater sense of scale for his images. Giusti's layout reflected his design philosophy–it was experimental, pushing the boundaries of magazine layout. Through a fine balance between the illustrations of his work and the additional visual elements, the artist created an intriguing, energized layout without overshadowing the artwork itself.

Though he seemed to have found ample clients in Switzerland, Giusti's attention was drawn to the United States in the late 1930s.

13 Quoted in Edward S. Morse, "The Man Who Signs His Work Giusti," CA: *The Magazine of the Communication Arts* (July/August 1965): 26, and in Ian Ball, "Faces in Metal," *Daily Telegraph Magazine* (May 25, 1972): 33.

14 Bert, 22; Authors' interview with Robert Giusti, August 27, 2014.

15 Authors' interview with Robert Giusti, August 27, 2014.

16 "Design Dossier: Giusti," 144; Morse, 28.

In part, he saw greater opportunities for a designer in the States than in Switzerland: "In Zurich, those days, there were as many designers as there were accounts."[13] But he also seems to have had larger concerns for his family. Giusti had married Margot Joachimsthal Reiche, a Berlin-born fashion designer and illustrator whom he met while they were both living in Switzerland. In 1937, the family grew larger with the birth of their son, Robert. Giusti made an initial trip to the United States to take on projects with the help of European colleagues, intending to stay only temporarily; but with concerns about the unrest and war in Europe, the Giusti family immigrated to the United States in 1938 aboard the ocean liner New Amsterdam.[14]

An Atmosphere of Complete Confidence: A New Foothold

Soon after Giusti arrived in the States, Herbert Matter, the Swiss designer who already had emigrated from Zurich to New York, put him in touch with the United States Census Bureau.[15] Giusti was commissioned to do a series of posters for the 1940 U.S. Census that were included in the 1939 and 1940 Golden Gate International Exposition in San Francisco, celebrating the completion of the Golden Gate Bridge and the San Francisco–Oakland Bay Bridge.[16] The series shared an affinity with other progressive design programs of the era, most notably ads being created for the Container Corporation of America by some of the best recent émigré designers, such as Matter, Herbert Bayer, and A. M. Cassandre. Giusti incorporated a simple, streamlined central image into each poster, with defining phrases beneath; yet the images were illustrative and easily understandable, a recognition of the broad, general audience the posters were meant to engage.

Giusti, one of a series of posters for the
1940 US Census designed for the 1939 and
1940 Golden Gate International Exposition in
San Francisco. Illustrated in "George Giusti,"
AD 7, no. 4 (April–May 1941): 7.

Giusti, Army Air Corps poster for
Museum of Modern Art competition, 1941,
illustrated in Georgine Oeri,
"George Giusti, Graphic Artist," *Graphis* 5,
no. 26 (1949): 151.

17 Giorgio Giusti, *New-York Book* no. 2,
October 28, 1938–September 1954, n.p.
Collection of Robert Giusti.

Giusti went on to collaborate with Herbert Matter
on the Swiss Pavilion for the 1939 World's Fair in New York,
for which Giusti prepared a series of displays.[17]

18 "Defense Posters Go on View Today," *New York Times*, July 16, 1941, 5. Giusti's US Army Air Corps poster was illustrated in Oeri, 151; See Giusti's poster "No medium bomber has a finer war record than your MITCHELL," 1943 Smithsonian National Air and Space Museum ID A19960381000.

19 David Lidman, "The World of Stamps: Abstract Design Slated for Fine-Arts Issue," *New York Times*, September 20, 1964, 27; Alvin Shuster, "Stamps for Art's Sake," *New York Times*, September 20, 1964, 30.

Giusti managed to participate in a number of officially sponsored public projects in his early years in America: He won an award of merit for his submission to a Museum of Modern Art national defense poster competition in 1941 (his was among 30 works chosen for display at MoMA), and he designed at least one poster for the U. S. Army Air Corps.[18] Giusti also completed a series of forest fire prevention posters (which were also issued as non-postage stamps) for the Forest Service in 1945. In each of the *Prevent Forest Fires* posters, Giusti again made simplified stylized elements the central focus of the composition, using scale to generate a visual hierarchy. Typography framed the image but was secondary to pictorial elements isolated in the dark backgrounds, elements that emphasized the human element, the cause of the problem and the potential solution, communicating quickly that prevention meant being more thoughtful with actions. Giusti occasionally designed actual stamps for the U. S. Postal Service, including a somewhat uninspired 1958 stamp commemorating the Atlantic Cable Centenary featuring Neptune, a mermaid, and a schematic globe bisected by a heavy horizontal line symbolizing the cable across the ocean. In 1971, he designed a stamped envelope with a spare, embossed, crimson and white design honoring bowling. Giusti was one of four finalists in a competition to design a 1964 stamp celebrating fine art, though a design by Stuart Davis was ultimately chosen. Giusti's design, compared to those of his fellow finalists Davis, Ben Shahn, and Robert Gwathmey, was harder-edged, less illustrational, and did not include obviously hand-rendered type. Giusti's spare flag design may have been inspired by Jasper Johns's flag paintings.[19]

Giusti, USDA Forest Service
Prevent Forest Fires!
non-postage stamp series, 1945.
From the collection of the Authors.

20 Giusti, letter and questionnaire about
Fortune sent to Phil Beard, December 22,
1984, 2. George Giusti Collection,
Cary Graphic Arts Collection at
The Wallace Center, Rochester Institute of
Technology. Giusti's account books show
cover design proposals for *Fortune* as early
as March 1939. Giusti, *New-York Book* no. 2,
October 28, 1938–September 1954, n.p.

21 Giusti, letter and questionnaire to
Phil Beard, 1. Giusti mistakenly identified
Peter Piening as "Walter Peening."

Giusti's biggest break in America came as he established a
long-standing relationship with *Fortune* magazine, becoming
one of an impressive fraternity of artists and designers who
worked for the magazine, among them Herbert Bayer,
A. M. Cassandre, Fernand Leger, Alvin Lustig, Matter, and
Charles Sheeler. "After a few months in the U.S.A," recalled
Giusti, "I prepared a small portfolio of my work which
I submitted to Francis Brennan [the art director at *Fortune*].
Soon after, he gave me my first assignment," the cover of the
February 1941 issue.[20] Brennan was the first of the *Fortune*
art directors Giusti worked with there–the others were
Peter Piening, Will Burtin, and Leo Lionni, all of whom
Giusti found to be excellent colleagues. Giusti recounted that
"*Fortune* was THE glamour magazine of that period. Working
with all the people involved was pleasant, relaxed and
of great value for the artist. In an atmosphere of complete
confidence the Art Director gave me 'carte blanche' for the
solution and technical execution of the problem involved."[21]

22 Giusti's son Robert, who would become an accomplished designer and illustrator himself, recalled spending hours as a young boy in the early 1940s in their apartment at 4445 Post Road in the Bronx watching his father design covers and posters with meticulous precision. Authors' interview with Robert Giusti, August 27, 2014; Nancy Tutko, "For New Milford Illustrator, Success Means Keeping Busy," *New York Times*, November 30, 1986, 43.

23 Watson, 15–6.

24 Giusti, letter and questionnaire to Phil Beard, 2.

The creative freedom of the *Fortune* projects suited Giusti well—his process had already developed to the point where he tended to visualize his final product without much need for preliminary sketches.[22] Giusti's early training focused on the importance of craft regardless of medium; the isolation and distillation of the subject and the precision of presentation served him well in his professional practice. Working almost exclusively in tempera topped sparingly with colored inks applied with an airbrush, Giusti was said to think out his designs "quite completely before beginning to paint. Usually no more than two or three rough pencil sketches precede his color comprehensive. This comprehensive is rendered with as much finish as his final painting."[23] Serendipitously, Giusti reported, "*Fortune* gave me TOTAL freedom. Most of the time I did not submit sketches—I delivered final artwork. I never had to modify anything."[24]

Giusti's early designs, such as his first *Fortune* covers and his wartime posters, offered a balance of specific detail and schematic fragmentation or abstraction. At a time when technology and industry were not only celebrated as tools of the United States's economic success but were also inextricably associated with the nation's ability to prevail in WWII, Giusti's visual articulation of engineering and applied science must have rung especially true for his clients and his audiences. Early observers related Giusti's boyhood ambition to be an engineer to the prevalence of technology in his designs. "Things mechanical continue to fascinate him," wrote Ernest Watson in 1943, "whether it is the anatomical structure of the human eye or the engine of an airplane. Such things he renders with perfect precision and an unusual feeling of reality within a pattern that is far from naturalistic...."

Giusti, cover for *Fortune*,
(February 1941).
George Giusti Collection,
Cary Graphic Arts
Collection at
The Wallace Center,
Rochester Institute
of Technology.
Fortune logo and
cover design © Time Inc.

Giusti, cover for *Fortune*,
(May 1948).
George Giusti Collection,
Cary Graphic Arts
Collection at
The Wallace Center,
Rochester Institute
of Technology.
Fortune logo and
cover design © Time Inc.

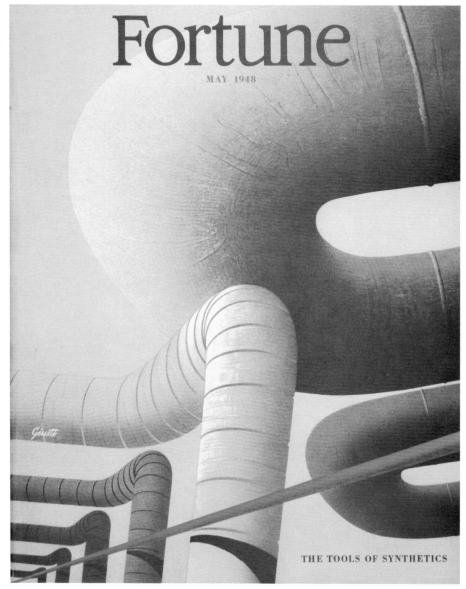

25 Watson, 15. This article was reprinted
   as Ernst Watson, "Giusti," in
   Forty Illustrators and How They Work
   (Ayer Company Publishers, 1946), 148–51.

More often than not, Giusti violates photographic perspective in order to achieve more-than-photographic reality."[25] Indeed, Giusti's early posters and covers for *Fortune* centered upon an abstract precision in which the visual attributes of his subject would be rendered with a sense of detail and volume while at the same clearly diverging from a simple, accurate illustration. In a style akin to that of Giusti's fellow *Fortune* cover artist, Precisionist Charles Sheeler, subtle variations of tonal values gave an almost photographic rendering of volume in objects such as a gun breech, but the forms were arranged subject to the geometries and juxtapositions of the composition rather than being a naturalistic representation of actual objects. Giusti was quite adept at synthesizing the visual information that could encapsulate the magazine's tribute to the industry of war.

Giusti's award-winning cover for the May 1948 issue of *Fortune* distilled the manufacture of synthetics into a striking composition that underscored the centrality of pipes in the production of products such as rayon and cellulose, but did not actually directly illustrate the industrial equipment. Will Burtin, who art-directed the project, outlined the process he worked through with Giusti: after they hit upon the theme, Giusti and Burtin clarified the composition, removed distracting details, and chose an appropriate palette. The design suggested manufacture of newly discovered chemicals through simplified geometric shapes, making the complex technology more accessible to a general audience. The cropped pipe forms created a fluid movement of elements through the illusionary space and activated the space beyond the edges of the cover.

Giusti, cover for
AD (April/May 1941).
George Giusti Collection,
Cary Graphic Arts Collection
at The Wallace Center,
Rochester Institute of Technology.

26 Will Burtin, "Award of Distinctive Merit to
  George Giusti for Magazine Cover Art,"
  Art Directors Club Annual (1948/9): 180–1.

The thin red straight pipe cutting dramatically through the lower portion of the composition, contrasted and balanced with the gray background and the more understated tones of the larger curving pipes. Given the generous size of *Fortune*, it seems appropriate that they conceived of the cover as "a poster, simple and easy to understand." Yet it also "must reveal textural values and details, which satisfy the initiated and provide new points of interest." Burtin continued, "The formula then, is Theme + poster approach + graphic detail = a magazine cover."[26] For many decades to come, Giusti would keep this poster-like approach to his magazine and book cover design, though his style would continuously evolve as his career progressed.

27 Authors' interview with Robert Giusti, August 27, 2014.

28 Giusti quoted in Allen Hurlburt, *The Design Concept: A Guide to Effective Graphic Communication* (New York: Watson-Guptill Publications, 1981), 88.

29 "Design Dossier: Giusti," 144.

When it seemed appropriate to the project, Giusti could tend toward an uncanny depiction of space and objects that revealed an affinity for the psychologically charged expanses of Surrealist painters. Covers he created for *The Studio* annual and the design journal AD suggest the dream-like landscapes of Giorgio de Chirico, whose work Giusti admired and emulated in early paintings.[27] In the AD cover (for an issue that included a spread featuring his work), Giusti created a series of symbols and references that conjured up associations with the international realm of commercial art: the flags, dollar sign, artist's tools, and hand connected to the journal title suggested the control of the art director. Yet odd features like the ominous black clouds, the disembodied hand with fingers splayed, and a large orb emblazoned with the title of the journal added a fantastic effect. As concise and pragmatic as Giusti could be, he valued creative imagination throughout his career; he said, "The idea of the work sprouts in some hidden corner of my ego where the subconscious holds sway. Logical considerations only start to come later, when I begin to give reality to the original idea and make it visible to others."[28] When given the latitude by a client like AD, he could free himself a bit from purely "logical considerations." Perhaps it was this sort of otherworldly quality that led a 1939 profile of Giusti to declare, "His sense of colour and the various techniques which he has mastered are proof of a rare ability in a graphic designer; his discipline as an artist and his understanding of psychology contribute to make him an advertising man with a future."[29]

30 Oeri, 148. "Georgine Oeri, Art Critic and Teacher, Dead at 54," *New York Times*, July 16, 1968, 39. Oeri wrote often for the seminal design journal *Graphis*, worked at the Guggenheim Museum as a lecturer, and shared an employer with Giusti when she served as an art consultant for the pharmaceutical company Geigy.

In fact, in addition to his work in posters and magazine covers, Giusti was making a name for himself in the realm of advertising–if not with his ability to create a psychologically charged image, then with his ability to visually synthesize complex concepts into intriguing visual language. Design critic Georgine Oeri observed in the late 1940s,

> While there is no gainsaying his marked talent for representing technical products, facts and processes in clear and unmistakable pictures (*Fortune* covers), that is perhaps not the essence of his work. The ability to present realities and to simplify forms down to an explicit minimum, backed by the will to a sensuous and almost obvious distinctness, does not derive, as one might first assume, from a belief in a fixed form of things, but springs from the imaginative power–strengthened, it is true, by a Latin sense of form–for embodying the unseen. Giusti is taken up with the discovery of pictures for things that are not accessible to the normal visual powers of the human eye. Jobs in which a pictorial interpretation has to be found for the revelations of modern science suit him and attract him, especially when–as with the Davison Chemical Corporation–he is completely free to go about the task as he thinks best.[30]

Between 1944 and 1950, Giusti completed nearly two dozen advertisements for the Davison Chemical Corporation as the company transitioned into the immediate post-WWII period. Giusti's ads touted the company's scientific innovations though a visual language that distilled the complexities of products, such as moisture-fighting desiccants and chemical fertilizers, to a message apprehensible to a general audience.

Giusti, silica gel advertisement,
the Davison Chemical Corporation,
1945. George Giusti Collection,
Cary Graphic Arts Collection
at The Wallace Center,
Rochester Institute of Technology.

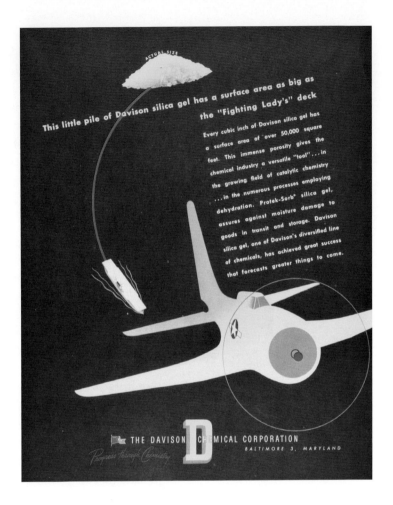

Building upon the celebration of wartime technology that had been a staple of *Fortune*, Giusti's ad touting Davison's silica gel referenced the 1944 film *The Fighting Lady*, a documentary about the aircraft carrier *uss Yorktown*, and featured a warplane sharply climbing with the ship far below. As in many of his Davison ads, Giusti isolated and simplified images to focus the narrative, and he used a stark background and solid black to enhance the colors used within the ad. Tilted text and the red line connecting a photograph of the silica gel to the image of the aircraft carrier created a sense of a kinetic energy, and the cropped wing of the plane suggested an extension beyond the frame of the ad. Giusti was careful to create a sense of visual coherence – the cantilevered text at the top aligned with the wings of the airplane, creating a symmetrical balance of compositional elements framing the body copy.

Faced with the task of devising ways to connect invisible chemical processes to appealing imagery for Davison, Giusti would often layer and juxtapose imagery of varied forms. For instance, he might layer diagrams of molecular structures atop recognizable images and abstract organic forms. In his ad for agricultural uses of phosphorous, Giusti created a directional narrative that illustrated the role of phosphorous in the production of food with illustrational and schematic images that suggested the cascading effect of enriched soil increasing plant growth, which in turn aided livestock, which in turn increased food production.

Giusti, "The Farmer is a Chemist"
advertisement,
the Davison Chemical Corporation,
1950. George Giusti Collection,
Cary Graphic Arts Collection
at The Wallace Center,
Rochester Institute of Technology.

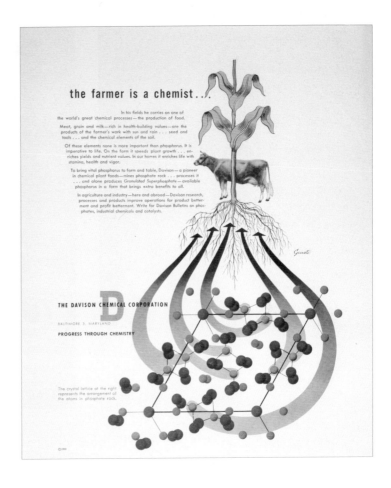

As in his work for Davison, Giusti's covers for *Vision*, the in-house journal of the American Optical Company, used photography, drawn objects, and graphic elements to create the feel of a functional schematic combined with visually engaging illustration. Giusti fashioned a system comprised of dreamlike deep spaces, either painted or photographic, in which he created a focal point, directing the viewer's eye and navigating through the message about American Optical's products that augmented vision.

Giusti, cover for *American Optical Vision*
[AO Training Gun Sight] 28, no. 2
(August 1944). George Giusti Collection,
Cary Graphic Arts Collection
at The Wallace Center,
Rochester Institute of Technology.
With permission of the
Optical Heritage Museum.

Giusti, cover for *American Optical Vision*
[AO Variable Density Goggle] 28, no. 3
(November 1944). George Giusti Collection,
Cary Graphic Arts Collection
at The Wallace Center,
Rochester Institute of Technology.
With permission of the
Optical Heritage Museum.

Giusti, cover for *American Optical Vision*
[New AO Monoplex Eye] 29, no. 1
(March 1945). George Giusti Collection,
Cary Graphic Arts Collection
at The Wallace Center,
Rochester Institute of Technology.
With permission of the
Optical Heritage Museum.

31 Special thanks to Dick Whitney of
Carl Zeiss Vision, Inc. for identifying the
bibliographic information for these issues
of *American Optical Vision*.

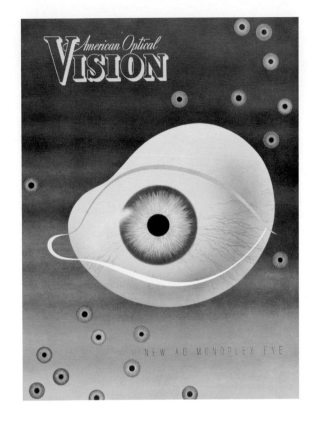

Incorporating illustrations of these products, contrasts of
light and dark, and plays of transparency and opacity,
Giusti engaged viewers directly with an eye pictured looking
straight at the viewer, and less directly through diagrams
of the act of spotting and targeting.[31] In these projects,
as with his AD cover, Giusti incorporated a bit of a surrealist
aesthetic–in the illusion of deep space, in the disembodied
eyes, and especially in the floating irises scattered across the
monoplex eye cover.

32 P. K. Thomajan, "George Giusti,"
  Graphis 59 (1955): 266. Giusti was a
  longtime friend of Walter Herdeg,
  the founder and editor of *Graphis*.
  R. Roger Remington, "Remembering
  George Giusti," *Graphis* 285
  (May–June 1993): 98.

33 Robert Goldwater and René d'Harnoncourt,
  "Modern Art in Your Life,"
  Bulletin of the Museum of Modern Art 17,
  no. 1 (1949): 3, 5–48.

34 Goldwater and d'Harnoncourt, 32.

Constantly Searching for New Approaches

In a 1955 profile published in *Graphis*, P. K. Thomajan echoed much of what Georgine Oeri had pointed out earlier, admiring Giusti's "quickened temperament" that was "attuned to this era of electronics and cybernetics, for which he is ideally equipped to act as an interpreter." Like Oeri before him, Thomajan saw in Giusti's work a practical application of the language and ideas of modern art: "The visual verities that he forges from new truths… reinforce the integrity of modern art. Giusti keeps himself unencumbered and untrammeled by the impedimenta of stolid tradition."[32] The varying degree of interconnectedness between modern art and design was given plenty of consideration at this time. In a 1949 exhibition and catalogue, the Museum of Modern Art pondered the interchange between what was perceived to be the rarified realm of modern art and the design of elements of everyday life.[33]

By the mid-1950s, Giusti had proven himself as an adaptive and evolving designer, one dedicated to concise visual communication but willing to expand and experiment stylistically. Giusti's 1952 cover for *Interiors* incorporates the mix of photographic materials, illustration, and painted forms he used in earlier ads, but the organic, bird-like shapes are less diagrammatic. The ever-experimenting Giusti was able to manifest his expanding stylistic repertoire on the cover of *Graphis* several times in the 1950s. For the cover of a 1952 issue, he featured the calligraphic lines of a wire sculpture of a boat mounted on a textured white gesso field that suggested a quick drawing. Museum of Modern Art curators Robert Goldwater and René d'Harnoncourt called the style Giusti adapted the "most characteristic of the twentieth century… the style of the wandering line."

Giusti, cover for *Interiors* (May 1952)
George Giusti Collection,
Cary Graphic Arts Collection
at The Wallace Center,
Rochester Institute of Technology.

Giusti, cover for *Graphis* 8, no. 43 (1952)
George Giusti Collection,
Cary Graphic Arts Collection
at The Wallace Center,
Rochester Institute of Technology.

Their description applies well to Giusti's cover image that is "apparently only aimless, but somehow emerges into a well-knit pattern; that is apparently only self-propelled, but also encloses form; that is apparently only abstract but does at least suggest representation; that is apparently spontaneous and thoughtless and yet achieves an extraordinary subtlety."[34] Only upon close examination did the form of Giusti's boat become apparent, as he explored an intermediary zone between abstraction and representation. That sense of calculated spontaneity and meaningful playfulness would characterize much of Giusti's work through the 1950s and into the 1960s.

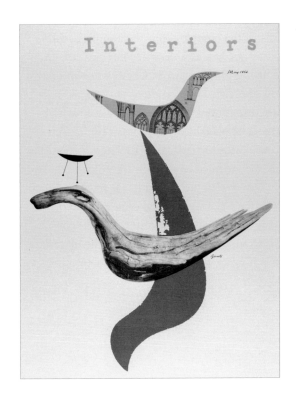

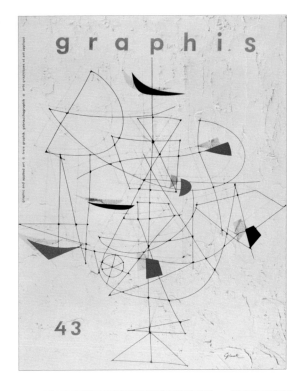

35 Quoted in Morse, 26.

36 Giusti, letter and questionnaire to Phil Beard, 1.

37 Authors' interview with Robert Giusti, August 27, 2014; Aubrey Simpson, "George Giusti," *Hemispheres* (October 1995): 13.

Giusti attributed some of his freedom to experiment and grow as a designer to the American context: "Over here," he wrote, "there is no feeling of 'shyness' on the part of modern designer. In this climate there is room for experimentation, for terrific mistakes and for unsurpassed achievements."[35] And Giusti retained this drive for innovative solutions to problems of visual communication throughout his career, writing in 1984, "It is part of my life philosophy to be constantly searching for new approaches. To me, The IDEA is the heart of the matter; than [sic] follows the visual solution, last comes technique."[36] These new approaches would lead him to new media and new techniques as he developed relationships with new clients.

Giusti's ability to distill the complex into the comprehensible informed his activities not just as a designer but as a design educator as well. Throughout his career, Giusti was thoughtful about the education of artists and designers. In 1944, he had published the instructional book *Drawing Figures*, in which he explained the rigors of his education in Italy, rigors that shed light on the foundations of his calculated and meticulous design process. Giusti continued to take on the role of educator, teaching creative design at Cooper Union in 1947.[37] For Giusti, teaching seemed to offer a gratifying level of self-consciousness and accountability; as he explained, the interconnectedness of concept, process, technique, and product, and the materials he developed for teaching offer invaluable insights into his own work.

38 Randy Kennedy, "The Draw of a Mail-Order Art School: Famous Artists Archives Go to the Norman Rockwell Museum," *New York Times*, March 23, 2014, A20.

39 Engel, n.p.

40 Letter outlining Giusti's responsibilities in developing curricula for the Famous Artists School, typewritten manuscript, November 5, 1959, 1–3, George Giusti Collection, Cary Graphic Arts Collection at The Wallace Center, Rochester Institute of Technology. These were specifics building on a contract that had been drawn up in 1958. Collection of Robert Giusti.

The apex of Giusti's career as an educator came in 1958, when he was recruited by the Famous Artists School to formulate their Graphic Design curriculum. Founded in 1948 by illustrator Albert Dorne, the correspondence school boasted curricula developed by well-known artists such as Norman Rockwell, Ben Shahn, and Stuart Davis.[38] In 1960, when the addition of Giusti to the faculty was announced, the school profiled him as "a superb draftsman in the traditional sense, he bases his work on the fundamental truths inherent in all art. He believes that it is through creative thinking, sound development, and stripped-to-the-bone simplicity that the designer's ideas achieve their fullest impact."[39]

Though Giusti probably did not have close contact with the students—most of the student correspondence seems to have been handled by lesser-known faculty—he clearly labored over the development of the lessons for the Famous Artists School. Giusti was contracted to formulate lessons on principles of practical and experimental design, advertising and editorial layout, and specialized design, and he contributed to other lessons related to his fields of expertise.[40] Illustrated with examples by Lester Beall, Will Burtin, Ivan Chermayeff and Thomas Geismar, William Golden, Leo Lionni, Alvin Lustig, Paul Rand, Reynold Ruffins, Ben Shahn, Bradbury Thompson, and, of course, himself, Giusti's lessons concisely synthesized principles of design informed by his core design philosophy. "Only by experimenting," he told the students, "can the designer escape the same old patterns and create fresh new concepts of layout and design that will capture the attention of readers.

41 Giusti, "Lesson 18: Experimental Design," *Famous Artists Course* (Westport, CT: Famous Artists School, Inc., 1960), 3.

If artists had not been willing to experiment, we would not have had the great and varied forms of art of the Egyptians, Greeks, Romans, the men of the Renaissance, and today's modern artists and countless artistic directions. It is the experimental artists who created the great art of the past and it will be the experimental artists who create the new trends of tomorrow." But, true to his respect for tradition, Giusti warned the young designer, "Your experiments in design should be based on a background of principles that have already proven their worth."[41]

Central to Giusti's message to his students, as it was to his own work, was finding the essence of the visual message, stripping away superfluous information that could muddle the communication of the central idea. "There is no substitute," explained Giusti, "for clean, simple, uncluttered design when you want to communicate an idea clearly. You can usually do this by removing every element which is not essential.... A symbol is the clearest way to present an idea and should be interpreted with originality, but still retain every characteristic that makes its message clear. With symbols the design never moves away from the subject. A symbol spells out the idea strongly and directly through the design." And, as he would in his own work, Giusti encouraged his students to appraise a problem thoroughly, assess the promise of a creative direction, and think it through to the end. "The time you spend considering the value of each approach is never wasted," he explained. "Actually it leads to a better and faster solution in the long run. I think all around the subject and ask, what is the main idea? What is the clearest way to express it? What is the best technique?... I ask, do all the elements of the design contribute to the meaning? Are there any jarring notes?

42   Quoted in Engel, n.p.

43   Giusti, "Lesson 19: Advertising
      and Editorial Design and Layout,"
      Famous Artists Course, 20–1.

Giusti, page spread for
"Lesson 18: Experimental Design,"
Famous Artists Course (Westport, CT:
Famous Artists School, Inc., 1960), 20–1.
George Giusti Collection,
Cary Graphic Arts Collection
at The Wallace Center,
Rochester Institute of Technology.

Can it be simplified?"[42] Using his 1958 cover for an issue of *Holiday* devoted to England, Giusti relayed how he took his original inspiration from an old engraving of the official British coat of arms that included a crowned lion. Through abstraction and simplification, Giusti isolated the lion and the crown to use them as powerful images that both represent royal associations with England and engage his more casual audience. He playfully cropped the lion and then systematically eliminated superfluous detail to create a composition of colorful planes of regal colors (mimicked in the type) and bold black shapes that gave the illustration a poster-like quality for newsstand impact.[43]

44 Giusti, "The Poster," handwritten draft for Famous Artists School lesson, c. 1959–60, 33. George Giusti Collection, Cary Graphic Arts Collection at The Wallace Center, Rochester Institute of Technology.

45 Giusti, "The Magazine Cover," handwritten draft for Famous Artists School lesson, 20 [version 2].

As he considered the curriculum that moved from one design application to the next, Giusti spelled out the communication challenges of each medium and why calculated simplicity was so crucial. Commenting on the poster, Giusti reasoned,

> The speed with which the poster has to communicate an idea is terrific, it has to be so fast, as to impress the passerby, that a special technique has to be employed. This technique we call "the punch into the eye." It sounds brutal, but nothing short of this particular quality can attract the attention of somebody concerned with the many distractions of the open road and of clustered city streets. Whatever a poster has to tell, or to sell, it has to do it quickly; whatever symbol the poster has to impress into the passerby, it can only do it if this symbol is stripped to bare essentials. In a poster, there is no room for romantic sentiment and overdone details…. Idea, conception, design, are the principle factors responsible in the efficiency of the poster.[44]

Moving on to magazine covers, Giusti wrote,

> The magazine cover is a poster in miniature. It has to have all the basic properties of the poster, meaning: the punch in the eye, the immediate power of communication for people on the run. In addition to that, since it will find its surroundings later in your own home, on the coffee table, on the magazine rack, it has to have the satisfying aesthetic properties of an artwork. The poster is the brasses of the orchestra; the magazine cover is the first violin; dignified but penetrating, leading, but not brutal! The magazine cover, in graphic arts, is the perfect medium for experimentation in textures and techniques.[45]

Giusti, original art
for the cover for *Fortune*
(September 1954).
George Giusti Collection,
Cary Graphic Arts Collection
at The Wallace Center,
Rochester Institute
of Technology.

Giusti, cover for
Modern Packaging
(February 1954).
George Giusti Collection,
Cary Graphic Arts Collection
at The Wallace Center,
Rochester Institute
of Technology.

Giusti, cover for
Modern Packaging
(May 1954).
George Giusti Collection
Cary Graphic Arts Collection
at The Wallace Center,
Rochester Institute
of Technology.

Giusti, cover for
Modern Packaging
(July 1954).
George Giusti Collection,
Cary Graphic Arts Collection
at The Wallace Center,
Rochester Institute
of Technology.

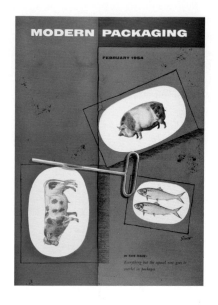

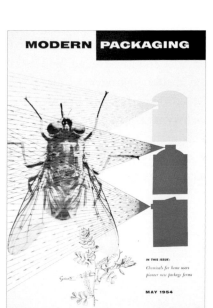

46 Beall appears to have found *Modern Packaging* too conservative at times. R. Roger Remington, *Lester Beall: Trailblazer of American Graphic Design* (New York: W. W. Norton & Company, 1996), 70.

When Giusti suggested to his students at the Famous Artists School that magazine covers were an ideal medium for experimentation, he was speaking from experience. Magazine covers continued to be a major focus of Giusti's attention in the 1950s. He continued to design covers for *Fortune* until 1954, working with art director Leo Lionni, and his style evolved from the precisely modeled volumetric forms of his earlier covers toward a looser collage aesthetic with a bolder, flatter, more abstract approach. This is evident in his final *Fortune* cover where the silhouette of a rearview mirror jutted into an unarticulated field of white. That same year, in 1954, Giusti had the unique opportunity to design every cover for the monthly magazine *Modern Packaging*, a publication that valued progressive design and in the 1950s often commissioned series of covers from standouts in the field of design, among them Lester Beall and Walter Allner.[46] Giusti's covers garnered international attention and revealed the range of his mid-1950s repertoire. His style used playful geometries and loose, hand-rendered illustrations alongside found images, photographs, and three-dimensional objects. Giusti created a system composed of a playful array of elements that allowed for an endless diversity of form while still maintaining a cohesive feel from one cover to the next. The hand-rendered lines and paint strokes brought a human element to the detail-laden photographs and found illustrations and to the modern typography.

Giusti, ad from the series
"Great Ideas of Western Man"
for the Container Corporation
of America, 1955.
George Giusti Collection,
Cary Graphic Arts Collection
at The Wallace Center,
Rochester Institute
of Technology.

47 Charles Coiner, "Pictures for Sales: A Group of Poster Artists Pushes at the Present Confines of the Medium," *Fortune* (August 1950): 90. The original ink and gouache art for Giusti's *Great Ideas* image was given to the Smithsonian American Art Museum by the Container Corporation of America (accession number 1984.124.107).

48 Michele H. Bogart, *Artists, Advertising, and the Borders of Art* (Chicago: University of Chicago Press, 1995), 157–70, 259–69.

The corporate appreciation for engaging design that was evident in the *Modern Packaging* covers was perhaps best manifested in the Container Corporation of America's decades of advertising. The Container Corporation showcased the work of many of the vanguard artists and designers of the day, often making little attempt to tout the actual products of the company. In 1950, designer and art director Charles Coiner, who was instrumental in developing the Container Corporation of America's ongoing embrace of fine art and design, illustrated a poster designed by Giusti as an example of work by 15 designers that push the limits of poster design, designers who included Herbert Bayer, Lester Beall, and Will Burtin.[47]

In 1955 Coiner recruited Giusti to contribute to the *Great Ideas of Western Man* series, which had begun in 1950 and would continue for over a quarter of a century.[48] Giusti was asked to create a visual counterpart to a quote by Jane Addams: "Civilization is a method of living, an attitude of equal respect for all men." As he described the projects for his Famous Art School students, Giusti explained that he had "almost complete freedom—the client insists only that that the work be unique, original, and in the best taste." He reported researching Addams to get a sense of her work and philosophy, and set himself to come up with a design that reflected her fight "against the prejudices aimed at the different races and creeds that make up America" and her belief "in the brotherhood of man—in equality for all regardless of race, creed or color of skin."

49 Giusti, "Lesson 19: Advertising
    and Editorial Design and Layout,"
    Famous Artists Course, 4–7.

He then illustrated a process of "thinking on paper" wherein he explored "a harmonious unity of races" through imagery of faces, figures with joined hands, and ultimately the formally and tonally balanced interlocking arms of the final piece (though for the original project, he probably simply thought these through and saved sketches for his most promising ideas).[49] In addition to the image of the interlocking arms, Giusti used the placement of type to direct the viewer's gaze clockwise around the illustration, ultimately drawing the eye into the focal point, the common ground of the diverse arms. This interplay of type and image created both a formal and a conceptual balance–the different-colored arms became one unit and depended on each other to complete the composition, an apt symbol of the message about humankind Giusti hoped to convey.

As he transitioned away from *Fortune*, Giusti began working regularly for the swanky, Philadelphia-based *Holiday* magazine. Through editor Ted Patrick's strategic recruitment of the era's best writers and photographers, the publication's stylish mix of travel writing and photography aimed at the status of literature and high art. The author contributors to *Holiday* included the likes of John Cheever, William Faulkner, Ernest Hemingway, Jack Kerouac, Carl Sandburg, John Steinbeck, and E. B. White. Photographic essays included projects commissioned from some of the most influential photographers bridging art and photojournalism of the day, among them, Henri Cartier-Bresson and Edward Steichen. *Holiday* was art directed by Frank Zachary, who had collaborated in 1949 with Alexey Brodovitch on *Portfolio*, a short-lived magazine that nonetheless managed to revolutionize magazine design.

50 Michael Callahan, "A Holiday for the
    Jet Set," *Vanity Fair* (May 2013): http://
    www.vanityfair.com/culture/2013/05/
    holiday-magazine-history.print.

51 Morse, 25.

52 "Frank Zachary, Editor and Art Director,
    Dies at 101," *New York Times*,
    June 13, 2015, A30.

53 Giusti quoted in Allner, 46.

54 Johnson, 46. Asger Jerrild, art director
    of the *Saturday Evening Post* (for which
    Giusti did illustrations and cover art
    in the mid-1960s), was another of the clients
    who was confident enough in Giusti to
    give him a great deal of creative latitude:
    "In all of his assignments he has always
    come up with a concept. I never tell him
    how I think it should be done. I'm careful
    not to put any limits on his thinking
    and I don't give him any musts. All I ask is
    that he develop his own concept."
    Quoted in Morse, 26.

Zachary recruited Giusti, who fashioned covers that expressed the discerning sophistication of the magazine's pioneering content. Giusti began working at *Holiday* during a period of great success for the magazine; its income doubled between 1954, the year of Giusti's first cover, and 1961. By the mid-1960s corporate cost-cutting had driven out many of *Holiday*'s editorial visionaries, including Zachary; yet Giusti managed to win commissions through the end of the decade.[50]

At *Holiday*, Giusti seemed to enjoy the same freedom and trust he had found at *Fortune*. As he assessed his collaborations with Giusti, Zachary; marveled, "If all the relationships between art director and artist were as tranquil as those with Giusti, there would be no need for tranquilizers. Giusti listens, almost immediately comprehends your problem, then goes about attaining the solution. Towards the later part of our relationship we found ourselves working with such complete understanding that it wasn't even necessary for him to come to the office. I'd call him on the telephone and explain the problem. When he came in, it would be with the final art."[51] Zachary and Giusti would continue to work together at other publications–Zachary was editor at *Travel & Leisure* and *Town & Country*–and Giusti designed covers for both publications in the 1970s and '80s.[52] Giusti certainly valued the partnerships with art directors such as Zachary that gave him the freedom to conceive and achieve his own solutions. Reflecting on less nurturing relationships, he recalled, "It has been my experience, a reaction shared by many colleagues in the profession, that the finest efforts are invariably rejected because clients lack vision in their judgment and confidence in the taste of the public. Thus, good ideas are strangled or else warped into lifeless submission by conventional straightjackets."[53]

Giusti, cover for *Holiday* (September 1957).
George Giusti Collection, Cary Graphic Arts
Collection at The Wallace Center,
Rochester Institute of Technology.

Giusti, cover for *Holiday* (April 1962).
George Giusti Collection, Cary Graphic Arts
Collection at The Wallace Center,
Rochester Institute of Technology.

And Giusti seems to have done his best to foster the sort
of relationship in which he would earn the respect of the
client and thus creative freedom. "With subtle diplomacy,"
Fridolf Johnson observed, "George Giusti never flaunts
his virtuosity as the expense of a client; he is an honest
workman in a field full of fakes, who really sells what his
client has to sell–with finesse and gusto."[54]

For many issues of *Holiday*, such as his April 1958 England issue, Giusti incorporated playfully simplified flat planes of color and bold graphics similar to those in his later *Fortune* work. In other covers for *Holiday*, Giusti employed the style he had been developing elsewhere in the 1950s, a style in which he also eschewed the fine lines and airbrushed modeling of his earlier work, giving way to looser, more calligraphic and painterly forms along with collaged elements. He relied less and less on illusionary space and mixed freely mingled painted and drawn components with photography and found images. His September 1957 *Holiday* cover featured wedge-shaped gray planes and a "2" built from roughly overlapping cutouts of illustrations, newspaper, and colored paper (the issue focused on Labor Day, which fell on the second of September that year). Giusti incorporated Picasso- and Schwitters-like collaged fragments to hint at the autumn buildup of events in the arts, music, television, sports, etc. The bold black central band read as an exclamation point and anchored snippets of fractured references to activities. The staggered vertical slivers that extended from top to bottom brought a sense of movement, energy, and anticipation to the composition and reiterated the bitonal treatment of the magazine title.

55 *SI63: 1963 Society of Illustrators Award Winners and Their Techniques* (New York: Society of Illustrators, 1963), n.p.

56 Johnson, 81. Johnson was a designer, calligrapher, typographer, and executive editor of *American Artist* from 1962 to 1970.

Though his style appeared more spontaneous, Giusti still stressed the idea of a fully thought-through solution to the design problem at hand. Commenting on his method of working, he described the making of the April 1962 cover for *Holiday*, featuring Washington, DC:

> It has been my practice over the years (Strength? Weakness?; I do not know) not to try to materialize my thoughts on paper until complete mental visualization is attained. So I train myself to see mentally. It is like passing a film in review: moving pictures changing, intermingling, taking shape and meaning. When a section of this imaginary film interests me, I hold it still, considering it further or rejecting it until I find the subject in shape I am seeking. Once I decide on the subject and I believe in its potentials, I don't let it go…. [In terms of the cover,] no drawings or sketches were made; the final artwork is the sketch. A portion of the Declaration (printed on newspaper) is pasted on illustration board. The eagle is painted with the quick single strokes of… transparent dyes.[55]

The lighter-hearted and seemingly spontaneous quality of Giusti's approach to *Holiday* and other projects of the era led critics to point out the sense of playful spontaneity in his designs. Fridolf Johnson, whose wife had known the Giustis since their days in Switzerland, wrote of Giusti's work, "His use of torn or cut paper and large brushes keeps his sketches simple, and he somehow manages to retain the same simplicity in the finished product. In fact, many of his designs look like his rough sketches, still glowing with the warmth of creation."[56]

57 Johnson, 46.

58 Johnson, 48.

59 Thomajan, 269.

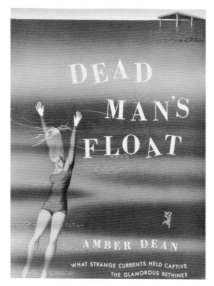

Giusti, cover for Amber Dean,
Dead Man's Float (Garden City, NY:
Doubleday Doran & Co., 1944).
George Giusti Collection,
Cary Graphic Arts Collection
at The Wallace Center,
Rochester Institute of Technology.

Johnson further noted, "His designs are disarmingly simple and look as if they were fun to do. At the same time, they leave no doubt as to their intended purpose: to communicate a certain feeling or atmosphere, to convey a thought, or to sell an idea or product."[57] Johnson attributed Giusti's mature style of the 1950s and early 1960s to his Italian heritage and education:

> In his designs are the broad hints of the sunny skies of Italy, his native land.... There he enjoyed in full measure his national heritage: a love of gay colors, music, and the rich folklore bequeathed to the Italian people by centuries of turbulent history. Through all his work there is woven these early-spun threads of color and fancy which knot themselves into evocative shapes and symbols that could be described as highly sophisticated folk art. Added to these is a subtle reflection of the refined taste and polish of an aristocratic ancestry. This interesting fusion of primitive force and elegant simplicity has been from the beginning an important ingredient in Giusti's concoctions.[58]

Commentators were quick to point out, however, that Giusti's sense of spontaneity was the result of the careful conception and forethought that he had always invested in his work. "Pristine prescience," wrote P. K. Thomajan in 1955, "that fine jewel of the subconscious, is what he prizes most. It enjoys psychic spontaneity which releases the inner springs of action. That is why this knowing designer makes every attempt to make his first sketch serve as his last."[59] In fact, Giusti's sketchbooks are an outstanding testimony to that assertion.

They are volume after volume of design after design, each idea almost fully finalized, rendered in precise lines and self-assured colors, a true testimony to the artist's thorough conceptualization, fine craftsmanship, and unrelenting discipline.

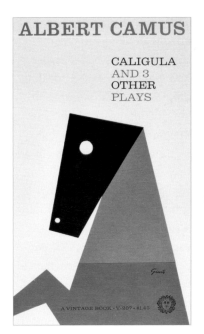

Giusti, cover for Albert Camus,
Caligula and 3 Other Plays
(New York: Vintage, 1958).
George Giusti Collection,
Cary Graphic Arts Collection
at The Wallace Center,
Rochester Institute of Technology.

Giusti, cover for Albert Camus,
Exile and the Kingdom
(New York: Vintage Books, 1958).
George Giusti Collection,
Cary Graphic Arts Collection
at The Wallace Center,
Rochester Institute of Technology.

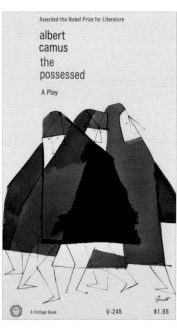

Giusti, cover for Albert Camus,
The Possessed: A Play in Three Parts
(New York: Vintage Books, 1960).
George Giusti Collection,
Cary Graphic Arts Collection
at The Wallace Center,
Rochester Institute of Technology.

60 See Ned Drew and Paul Sternberger, *By Its Cover: Modern American Book Cover Design* (New York: Princeton Architectural Press, 2005); Drew and Sternberger, *Purity of Aim: The Book Jackets of Alvin Lustig* (Rochester, NY: Rochester Institute of Technology Cary Graphic Arts Press, 2010); Steven Heller, "When Paperbacks Went Highbrow–Modern Cover Design in the 50s and 60s," *Baseline* 43 (2004): 5–12.

61 Giusti, "The Art Directors Club of New York," *Graphis* 17, no. 98 (November 1, 1961): 475.

62 Authors' interview with Robert Giusti, November 25, 2003.

From the late 1940s through the mid-1970s, Giusti frequently designed book covers for Anchor, Dolphin Books, Random House, and Vintage Books, his style ranging from the illustrative covers of the 1940s to the "big book look" of the 1970s. This was a period when book cover design flourished, especially in paperbacks, as mainstream publishers followed in the footsteps of groundbreaking presses such as New Directions, soliciting cutting-edge designers to create compelling graphic voices for their books.[60] As in his earlier work in advertising, Giusti excelled in what he called "dealing with intangibles," synthesizing complex abstract concepts into legible but engaging designs.[61] Thus, the majority of his book cover commissions were for publications focusing on subjects in the sciences and social sciences, though he did do some work for more literary subjects, including several American editions of works by Albert Camus. Allotted a good deal of creative latitude, Giusti created concise graphic distillations of complex philosophical and scientific book subjects.[62] For a cover of a book in the Science Study Series, *Cloud Physics and Cloud Seeding*, Giusti created a cross section of a cloud to schematize the process of cloud activity. Through seemingly simple use of line, color, scale, and weight, Giusti distilled the temporal and physical aspects of the process into a single illustration. Linear and planar forms denoted visible natural elements such as earth, land, and water while also suggesting less visible cyclical phenomenon such as airflow, evaporation, and condensation. Giusti was just as adept at creating diagrammatic visualizations of social phenomena. In conceiving his cover for *Interaction Ritual*, Giusti incorporated a Cubist-inspired juxtaposition of simplified heads and layered planes, with striking formal contrasts suggesting deeper processes of human interaction.

The flat yellow square with the profile played off the more organically shaped black planes of the frontal view with its wavy modulation that suggests volume. Solid lines served as a foil to dotted lines, yet they connected to create a sense of unity in the figure, and the crosshair-like eye seemed soulless, while the more naturalistic eye seemed more human.

Giusti, cover for Louis J. Battan, *Cloud Physics and Cloud Seeding* (Garden City, NY: Anchor Books, 1962). George Giusti Collection, Cary Graphic Arts Collection at The Wallace Center, Rochester Institute of Technology.

Giusti, cover for Erving Goffman, *Interaction Ritual: Essays on Face-to-Face Behavior* (Garden City, NY: Anchor Books, 1967). George Giusti Collection, Cary Graphic Arts Collection at The Wallace Center, Rochester Institute of Technology.

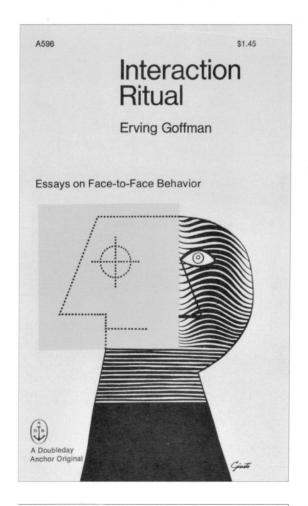

Sketch for spread from George Giusti and Rudolf Hoffmann, *Heart: Anatomy, Function and Diseases* (New York: Dell Publishing Company, 1962. George Giusti Collection, Cary Graphic Arts Collection at The Wallace Center, Rochester Institute of Technology.

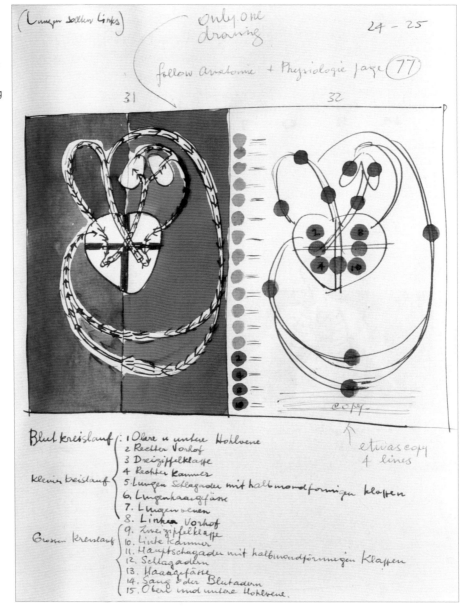

63 "New Development in Paperbacks," *Boston Globe*, April 1, 1962, 24A; "Scanning the Paperbacks," *Chicago Daily Tribune*, August 5, 1962, D7; Robert R. Kirsch, "The Book Report: Author, Artist Collaborate in Paperback Collection," *Los Angeles Times*, March 27, 1962, C5. Giusti's friend and colleague Gottfried Honegger was one of the authors of another in the series, *Space: The Architecture of the Universe*.

64 Authors' interviews with Robert Giusti, August 27, 2014, and August 28, 2015; John S. Wilson, "Enoch Light, Leader of a Big Band, Stereo Recording Innovator, Dead: Learned Business as Salesman," *New York Times*, August 1, 1978, B2.

Although most of Giusti's work for book publishing houses was cover design, he did occasionally illustrate entire books. In 1962, Dell published a series of "Visual Books" exploring subjects "of universal scope," and Giusti collaborated with Rudolf Hoffman, M.D., on *Heart: Anatomy, Function and Diseases*. The integration of image and idea in the series was heralded by some as groundbreaking–"a brilliant wedding of text and picture;" a true "collaboration of artist and authority."[63] Here Giusti was faced with the visualization of not only the physical processes of the circulatory system and its ailments, but also numerical and statistical information. To make the information comprehensible to a general audience, Giusti created a flow of abstract, simplified, and sometimes playful imagery that resembled a storyboard, each illustration building upon the next and augmenting the information in the text. Rich, vibrant colors played off one another, at once illustrating the concepts of the book and keeping the reader engaged as the sequences progressed.

Visualizing Music

In addition to creating covers for magazines and books, Giusti also designed dozens of record album covers in the 1960s for Command Records, a technologically innovative label founded by his friend Enoch Light.[64] Under the art direction of Charles E. Murphy, Command was dedicated to innovative design, employing not just Giusti but also many of the well-established and up-and-coming progressive designers of the day, including Joseph Albers and Walter Allner, as well as Ivan Chermayeff and Thomas Geismar.

Giusti playing guitar with his wife Margot, April 1945
Photograph from the Collection of Robert Giusti

Giusti, cover for Tony Mottola,
Guitar USA (Command Records, 1966).
George Giusti Collection,
Cary Graphic Arts Collection
at The Wallace Center,
Rochester Institute of Technology.

Giusti, cover for Enoch Light
and the Light Brigade,
A New Concept of Great Cole Porter Songs
(Command Records, 1962).
George Giusti Collection,
Cary Graphic Arts Collection
at The Wallace Center,
Rochester Institute of Technology.

Many of Giusti's covers featured his collage-like style of the period, using bold veils and planes of color to create imagery that echoed not just the albums' themes, but also the rhythms and syncopations of the music itself. In his cover for Tony Mottola's *Guitar USA*, Giusti's linear contours echoed the hovering bold yellow, black, and red planes of the guitar, creating a feeling of gyration with the rhythm and energy of the album, a visual embodiment of the music. In *A New Concept of Great Cole Porter Songs*, tilting, layered letterforms shifting in hue implied a dancing, moving crowd. The viewer was drawn into the center of the composition, the darkest and most dense area, where outlines and translucent versions of the melded "c" and "p" forms were most intensely layered.

65 Bert, 26; Authors' interview with
   Robert Giusti, August 27, 2014.

66 "Segovia in Action A Blending of Arts,"
   New York Herald Tribune,
   April 30, 1961, D15.

67 Bert, 22–3.

68 Morse, 28.

69 Special thanks to Jayson Dobney,
   Associate Curator and Administrator in the
   Department of Musical Instruments at the
   Metropolitan Museum of Art, for helping us
   with the correct names of these instruments.

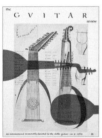

Giusti, cover for *Guitar Review*, no. 9, (1949).
George Giusti Collection,
Cary Graphic Arts Collection
at The Wallace Center,
Rochester Institute of Technology.

Giusti, cover for *Guitar Review* 31 (May 1969).
George Giusti Collection,
Cary Graphic Arts Collection
at The Wallace Center,
Rochester Institute of Technology.

Giusti's relationship with Command Records was a reflection of a larger, long-time passion for music, a passion that was focused particularly on the guitar. Giusti was introduced to classical guitar by Ukrainian émigré and illustrator Vladimir Bobri. He started lessons with classical guitarist Chauncey Lee and joined the New York Society of Classical Guitar, which had been formed by Bobri in 1936. The Society was a group with tight creative and social bonds. They would meet at La Zambra, a restaurant in midtown Manhattan (for which Giusti designed a mural) owned by flamenco guitarist and Giusti friend Vicente Gomez. And they would go to Romani guitarist Mirko Balsaldella's club, where famous guitarists, including Andrés Segovia (whom Giusti would also befriend), would stop by for informal performances.[65] In 1961 the Society of Classical Guitar held an event at which Segovia played while 20 artists, including Giusti, sketched him.[66] In the years following WWII, Giusti worked with fellow illustrators and designers and amateur guitarists Bobri, Gregory d'Alessio, and Antonio Petruccelli, to design and produce the first issue of *Guitar Review* in 1946.[67] With Bobri as art director and covers by the likes of Giusti, Frank Zachary called *Guitar Review* "the best designed small magazine in America."[68]

Giusti continued to design covers and create interior illustrations for *Guitar Review* until the late 1980s, revealing his experimentation in a vast range of styles, from a 1949 issue featuring a lute and a theorbo in a historical illustration and deep red overlaid silhouettes, to his May 1969 cover with a portrait of French composer and classical guitarist Ida Presti rendered in the elegantly simple line drawing style that Giusti often used in illustrations for the magazine.[69]

70 Giusti, letter and questionnaire to Phil Beard, 2.

71 William B. McDonald, "Geigy Chemical Corporation, USA: An Example of Integrated Advertising," *Graphis* 121 (1965): 396–403.

72 "Graphics at Geigy," *Industrial Design* 5 (1965): 32–4.

73 Bert, 25; Authors' interview with Robert Giusti, August 27, 2014.

74 Heller, "Fred Troller, 71, Champion of Bold Graphic Style," *New York Times*, October 24, 2002.

75 Morse, 28.

Giusti, Geigy Tanderil design,
c. mid-1960s.
George Giusti Collection,
Cary Graphic Arts Collection
at The Wallace Center,
Rochester Institute of Technology.

Giusti, Geigy Hygroton packaging,
c. 1960–3.
George Giusti Collection,
Cary Graphic Arts Collection
at The Wallace Center,
Rochester Institute of Technology.

Swiss Rigor Meets American Vitality

From 1960 to 1967, Giusti held a special position at J. R. Geigy, a Swiss corporation that traced its roots in textile dye, chemical, and drug manufacturing back to the eighteenth century. By the 1940s, Geigy had begun to establish itself among the great corporate patrons of innovative modern design alongside the likes of Container Corporation of America, IBM, and Braun. Giusti would play a pivotal role in Geigy's development of a design program in the United States, and assessing the trajectory of his career in 1984, Giusti saw his contract as art consultant for Geigy as the culmination of prominent assignments that had their roots in the exposure his *Fortune* covers had given him.[70]

Building on a firm foundation put together during the 1950s in Basel, Geigy's USA design team, headed by Swiss designer Fred Troller, was seen as a prime example of excellence in design: Talented designers not only fashioned identities for particular products but also envisioned an overall image for the corporation as a whole.[71] The design group, based at the company's Ardsley, New York complex, served all of the American divisions–Industrial, Chemical, Agricultural Chemicals, Dyestuffs, and Pharmaceuticals–though 85% of their work focused on Pharmaceuticals.[72] Troller was appointed art director of the USA design group in 1960 by Geigy Basel veteran artist/illustrator Gottfried Honegger, a friend of Giusti whose paintings Giusti collected.[73] Honegger understood the Swiss aesthetic, but also brought a cosmopolitan open-mindedness to the group that was reflected in his choice of Troller to head the American branch. Massimo Vignelli extolled Troller's work that "successfully combined Swiss rigorousness with American vitality."[74]

Giusti, too, seemed intent on enlivening Swiss rigor: In 1965, Edward S. Morse summarized Giusti's take on European design, explaining, "The American designer, in contrast to the European, works with greater courage, expressing his imagination more freely. European designers, and especially Swiss, he considers are masterful with typography, layout and printing processes. He finds them modern in their treatment, but feels that they tend to be somewhat stiff and neat, shying away from what might be considered experimental."[75] Some of Giusti's designs for Geigy reflected the enlivened yet refined Swiss aesthetic of many of the company's products, as in his graphics for Tanderil (a drug for the treatment of rheumatic diseases) with their late modernist grid structure and sans serif type. He achieved a clear hierarchy of image and information through scale, weight, space, and alignments. In Giusti's packaging for the anti-hypertension drug Hygroton, the physical ailment the drug was meant to treat was masterfully communicated in a powerful, clean aesthetic. A simple symbol illustrated the function of the drug in a manner that is at once abstract and accessible: an "H" with its jagged descending cross bar over a field of red suggesting a graph of lowered blood pressure.

The young designers at Ardsley were both Swiss and American and tended to have broader artistic sensibilities–Troller, for instance, made and exhibited paintings and sculptures in New York galleries. Geigy USA as a whole, seems to have been devoted to the same sort of broad artistic dedication. Honegger persuaded the art-savvy Geigy USA CEO Carl A. Suter to build a corporate collection of art, beginning with a painting by Franz Kline. With the help with another Basel transplant, critic and Guggenheim curator Georgine Oeri, Geigy USA acquired the core of their collection: twelve abstract works by American

76 Karen Gimmi, "Geigy Graphic Design
in the United States," in
*Corporate Diversity: Swiss Graphic Design
and Advertising by Geigy, 1940–1970*, ed.
Andres Janser and Barbara Junod
(Zürich: Museum für Gestaltung and
Lars Müller Publishers, 2009), 61–5.

77 Giusti, "Report on Art Department
Operation, Geigy Chemical Corporation,"
Ardsley, New York, Submitted by
George Giusti, Art Consultant,
December 21, 1961," typewritten manuscript,
n.p. George Giusti Collection,
Cary Graphic Arts Collection
at The Wallace Center,
Rochester Institute of Technology.

78 Giusti, "The Art Directors Club of
New York," 475.

79 Giusti, "Report on Art Department
Operation, Geigy Chemical Corporation," n.p.

80 Gimmi, 61–5.

81 Giusti, "Report on 1963–64 Propaganda
Material," typewritten manuscript,
July 1964, 5. George Giusti Collection,
Cary Graphic Arts Collection
at The Wallace Center,
Rochester Institute of Technology.

and Swiss artists. These works were purchased to grace the walls of the complex at Ardsley, which itself was a testimony to progressive design. In the late 1950s, Suter commissioned Skidmore, Owings & Merrill to create a sprawling series of offices and laboratories in glass and steel volumes contrasted with rustic stone bases.[76]

Beyond the regular design team at Ardsley, Giusti held a special position as an art consultant, an external advisor whose role was, as Giusti himself put it, to give "creative design direction to Geigy and its products." Giusti saw his principal task as "evolving symbols and devices that will spearhead the significance of both new and existing products." He suggested that he be included in all lines of communication from all the various departments and divisions at Geigy, including sales and budgeting, allowing him to have a sense of the company as a whole at any given time. Though an outside consultant, he positioned himself as an art director, suggesting weekly meetings in his private office, during which "work would be reviewed, new projects and strategies planned followed by distribution of assignments."[77]

Assessing the current state of Geigy design in America in 1962, Giusti saw the need for "a more ordered simplicity" and a lighter, more refined use of typography in Geigy's designs. Although in general Giusti admired an "appealing saliency" in which "packages had an institutional look that gave stature to an entire line,"[78] he looked for ways to humanize Geigy designs and copy, arguing, "People attract people. There is a persistent reticence in using such expressive elements as faces, figures and hands in printed matter. The use of purposeful art and photographs would quicken the appeal of Geigy literature."

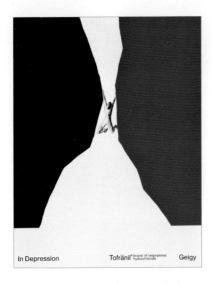

In Depression   Tofrānil® brand of imipramine hydrochloride   Geigy

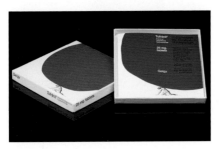

Giusti, Geigy Tofranil designs, c. mid-1960s.
George Giusti Collection,
Cary Graphic Arts Collection
at The Wallace Center,
Rochester Institute of Technology.

As for the copy at Geigy, Giusti maintained that it appeared to be "stilted and impersonal instead of intimate and ingratiating. It could well relax into a conversational tone, thereby accelerating communication...." Because he was "assuming responsibility for the Geigy look," he requested that he be consulted about "all matters pertaining to the company's appearance—architectural plans, interior decoration, etc. Thus there would be no lapses in maintaining an overall harmony of meaningful design."[79] Giusti's contributions to Geigy evolved well beyond consulting on Ardsley projects to include an impressive body of his own work for Geigy's international markets.[80]

In 1964, Giusti suggested that the campaign for the antidepressant Tofranil be "led gently into other directions," including perhaps "a series showing the struggle of the depressed patient, unable to cope with situations caracteristic [sic] of our modern life, etc."[81] Giusti's idea for the redirection was a series of images that pictured a figure in physically precarious situations that suggested the inner struggle with depression. Combining vast planes of color with purposeful white space and simple line drawings of figures, Giusti incorporated basic compositional principles such as scale, tension, and weight to visually communicate intense sensations associated with depression: stress, loss of control, and overwhelming anxiety. Continuing his quest to humanize Geigy campaigns, Giusti created designs for another antidepressant, Pertofrane, that incorporated minimal contrasting colors and layered, simple transparent figures to create a narrative of transformation and release from the grip of depression.

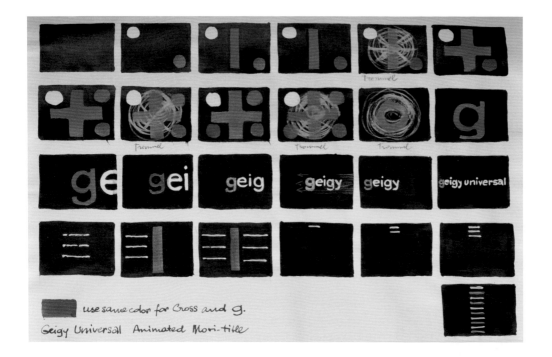

use same color for Cross and g.
Geigy Universal Animated Mori-title

82 Yvonne Zimmermann, "Target Group Oriented Corporate Communication– Geigy Films," in *Corporate Diversity*, ed. Janser and Junod, 49–57.

Beyond contributing to the thoughtful design of its packaging and advertising, Geigy had been making films to promote its products since 1939, using a marketing practice that many industries had been employing since early in the twentieth century. In the later 1940s and 1950s, Geigy's promotional films reached general audiences in Swiss movie theaters and in traveling cinema trucks, but by the 1960s they had switched to television spots. Into the 1960s, Geigy also focused on making films for specialized audiences and internal communications, including regularly produced installments of *Documenta Geigy*, a series of continuing education films for physicians, and *Geigy Universal*, films that explored aspects of the company's broad spectrum of activities in its many divisions.[82]

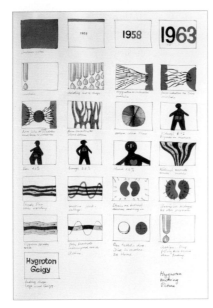

Giusti, Geigy film sequence
for Hygroton, c. 1963.
George Giusti Collection,
Cary Graphic Arts Collection
at The Wallace Center,
Rochester Institute of Technology. (Above)

Giusti, Geigy film title sequence, c. 1962.
George Giusti Collection,
Cary Graphic Arts Collection
at The Wallace Center,
Rochester Institute of Technology. (Left)

Giusti's unrealized film title sequence from about 1962 was conceived to accompany an installment of one of the films in the *Geigy Universal* series. Primarily a typographic solution, Giusti's abstracted forms of dots, lines, circles, and a cross (reminiscent of the Red Cross) evolved into the Geigy logotype.

Giusti's storyboard of a film about Hygroton, a water reduction drug to treat hypertension, began with a curtain rising to reveal a progression of years through scale and placement in the frame, referring to ten years of the drug's development. The imagery then shifted to a water drop that quickly multiplied, setting the stage for the journey of water through the body. Giusti then incorporated diagrams to illustrate the function of the drug in the body, its effects, and how its action differed from that of its competitors. Bold colors such as pinks, reds, and blues illustrated body systems and organs, and arrows indicated direction and movement. Vibrant yellow was a stark contrast to the earlier illustrations and brought into focus the primary differentiator of the drug– uninterrupted urine flow that reduced strain on the kidneys. Finally, Giusti built visual connections between the pill and the clock, bringing the narrative full circle, back to the water drop and time. This sequence reflected a number of Giusti's design concerns in his work at Geigy and beyond: He humanized the effects of the drug with figurative imagery; he combined text and image in engaging ways; and he created apprehensible visualizations of complex medical processes. The shifting imagery of the film sequence must have been an intriguing challenge to Giusti, who had described his creative process using a film analogy: images developing and shifting in his mind, coming to a stop when he hit upon a promising idea.

83 Giusti, "Report on Art Department Operation," n.p.

84 Janser and Junod, 194.

85 Giusti, "Report on 1963–64 Propaganda Material," 7.

Giusti saw design as a primary element in defining not just the look of Geigy but also the ideals of the company. Echoing grand projects like the Container Corporation's *Great Ideas of Western Man* series, Giusti proposed a "cultural ethical increment" in the "slow and steady development of a series of Geigy monographs that would serve to spell out Geigy ideas and ideals." But for Giusti the ideals of the company would not reflect simply the production of chemicals and pharmaceuticals, but rather go further to explore the nature of design and visual communication. "A typical title," he explained, "would be one devoted to the history of symbols, which represent the most elemental and vital form of communication. The thoughtful design of these documents would have considerable cumulative impact in high places."[83]

For Giusti, the closest thing to this sort of project at Geigy in America was the company's *Catalyst*, an in-house magazine that probably first appeared in the late 1950s and was published at irregular intervals over the course of the 1960s, with one designer from the design team responsible for the graphic conceptualization of each issue.[84] *Catalyst*, Giusti declared as he critiqued the 1963–4 graphic programs at Geigy, "is a consistently good example of fine conception, graphically and otherwise. The presentation is superb and the material interesting." But he longed for a grander audience: "I wish the budget would allow an expantion [sic] of literature of this kind and would permit the creation of a house magazine for outside consumption. It would be a fine way to spread the Gospel and make universally known the high aims of Geigy."[85]

Giusti's Geigy projects most often worked within the company's aesthetic of simple graphics and unmodulated planes of flat color. By the 1970s, Giusti had added a simpler, bold planar style punctuated by fine drawn lines to other facets of his graphic work, especially in some of the covers and illustrations he completed for broad-audience publications such as *Time*, *TV Guide*, and *Travel + Leisure*. Now incorporating bolder, warmer colors often associated with the 1970s, Giusti composed covers that at times shared an aesthetic with Pop Art. The flat planes of color and bold black contours of his 1969 *Time* cover featuring Ralph Nader were similar to Andy Warhol silkscreens, and his segmented jumbo jet with Ben-Day dots on a 1970 cover recalled the comic book-inspired work of artists such as Roy Lichtenstein. Most *TV Guide* covers of the era were publicity photographs for current television shows, but the magazine turned to Giusti for special issues, and they often asked him to do interior illustrations as well. Often using a text-as-image approach to the graphics, Giusti combined hand-rendered lettering with line drawn illustrations, as in his 1977 Fall Preview cover with its leafless tree emerging from the "L" of "fall" or diagrammatic symbols, and in the frenetic overlapping curved arrows behind the purple-shadowed bubble letters of "turmoil" in a 1974 cover.

Working for mass-market magazines such as *TV Guide* and *Time*, Giusti seems to have had less creative freedom than he had with earlier publications, probably reflecting changes in the publishing world as a whole. Though he reported that he had been able to submit finished designs to art directors at publications such as *Fortune* and *Holiday*, at *Time* he appears to have had to pitch his designs and compete with other designers.

86 Jerry Alten, letter to Giusti,
March 10, 1978.
George Giusti Collection,
Cary Graphic Arts Collection
at The Wallace Center,
Rochester Institute of Technology.

For instance, Giusti created at least four distinct designs for a 1968 cover, but ultimately the magazine went with a much more conservative cover by a different designer. Similarly, at TV *Guide*, Giusti seems to have had less freedom than he'd had with publishers earlier in his career, often submitting several versions of a cover. In response to Giusti's "too far out" graphics in the movies section of a 1978 Preview Issue, for instance, art director Jerry Alten asked for "something more conventional in the way of a movie cliché... the word 'movies' against a space background with spaceships coming out of the 'o' or something of that nature."[86] In some ways, Giusti's work for these broad audience publications with more intrusive art directors is more of a testimony to his innovative design vision than his work for earlier clients such as *Holiday* and *Modern Packaging*. In his work for publications such as *Time* and TV *Guide*, Giusti was able to balance his clients' demands with his own high standards for well-conceived and inventive designs. He managed to give his clients what they wanted, keep them coming back, and at the same time nurture his ever-evolving exploration of design.

A Vast Flux in Approaches

In the 1960s and '70s, in addition to work with bold, flattened areas of color, Giusti had also been evolving a large body of work that had a sculptural quality, apparently evolving from experiments with volumetric forms and collage conducted since the early decades of Giusti's career. By the 1940s this quality had been identified by Georgine Oeri, who wrote, "It would be difficult to find among Giusti's compositions one which does not contain this specific sense of space, an indefinable and ubiquitous spatial consciousness that awakens the same space-feeling in the observer.

Giusti, *Ralph Nader*, original art for the cover of *Time* (December 12, 1969). National Portrait Gallery, Smithsonian Institution; gift of *Time* magazine.

Giusti, *Najeeb E. Halaby*, original art for the cover of *Time* (January 19, 1970). National Portrait Gallery, Smithsonian Institution; gift of *Time* magazine.

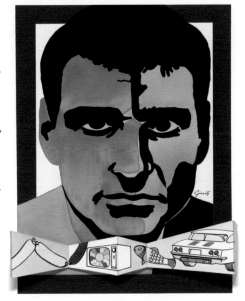

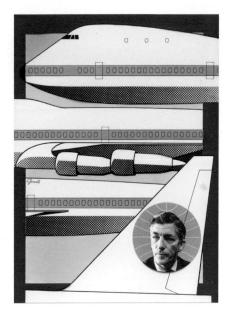

Giusti, cover for *TV Guide* (September 7–13, 1974). George Giusti Collection, Cary Graphic Arts Collection at The Wallace Center, Rochester Institute of Technology.

Giusti, cover for *TV Guide* (July 23–29, 1977). George Giusti Collection, Cary Graphic Arts Collection at The Wallace Center, Rochester Institute of Technology.

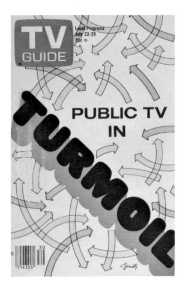

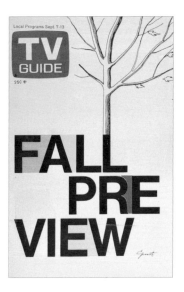

Giusti bends space as it were about its own axis. In doing so he satisfies both his own imagination and the demands imposed by the technical and scientific enterprises that commission his work."[87] Oeri was referring to the plays of space such as Giusti's manipulation of volumetric forms in his *Fortune* covers, his layering of imagery in his Davison ads, and the uncanny surrealist space in some of his other work; but by the early 1950s, Giusti's dialog between two and three dimensions had become even more direct. When working with more adventuresome clients, he created shallow sculptures that served as the basis for two-dimensional designs, giving a sense of depth and spatial play in his compositions. In 1952, he had designed the *Graphis* cover with an abstracted wire sculpture of a boat mounted on a textured white gesso field. And several of his 1954 *Modern Packaging* covers included not just collages of found images, planes of color, and drawn elements, but also actual objects laid on top of the collages and photographed for the final artwork.

By the 1960s, the creation of sculptural elements to be photographed as part of cover and advertisement designs had become a staple of Giusti's oeuvre. Although he often cut out layers of paper and board to build shallow three-dimensional constructions, as in his 1963–4 *Graphis Annual*, Giusti favored sheet metal in many of his designs. In his October 1964 cover for a *Holiday* issue featuring Germany, for instance, Giusti fashioned an abstract eagle from planes of colored paper and sheet metal that looked as if they were floating above the background and cast shadows, creating a sense of three-dimensionality.

Giusti, cover for *Holiday*
(October 1964).
George Giusti Collection,
Cary Graphic Arts
Collection at
The Wallace Center,
Rochester Institute
of Technology.

Giusti, cover for *Holiday*
(June 1966).
George Giusti Collection,
Cary Graphic Arts
Collection at
The Wallace Center,
Rochester Institute
of Technology.

88 Giusti's steel and
    aluminum sculpture of
    Willy Brandt that was
    used for *Time*'s 1970
    Man of the Year cover
    was included in an
    exhibition of *Time* cover
    portraits at the Smithsonian
    National Portrait Gallery
    in 1978 and was one of
    at least 17 pieces of original
    art by Giusti that was given
    to the museum by *Time*.
    Connie Lauerman, "Time
    and Time Again, Faces
    Cover News of the Day,"
    Chicago Tribune,
    May 18, 1978, A2. See
    http://npgportraits.si.edu
    for specifics of the National
    Portrait Gallery's holdings.

89 Giusti, letter
    and questionnaire
    to Phil Beard, 1.

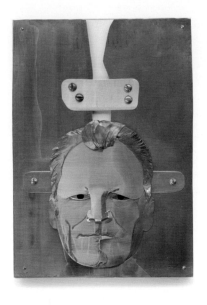

His covers for the 1966 Zambia issue of *Holiday* featured metal in a mask-like construction that incorporated curved and perforated planes of metal that amplified the three-dimensional effect.

By the late 1960s, Giusti was applying this sculptural technique to more general audience publications and advertising designs as well. For about a decade, beginning in 1967, Giusti designed over a dozen covers for *Time* magazine, including a January 1970 Man of the Year cover that featured his metal sculpture of Willy Brandt.[88] Planes of carefully cut, incised, and bent sheet metal made up the planes of the figure's face, with contrasting flame-oxidized sheet metal representing hair. As he did with many of his metal constructions, Giusti included hardware holding the piece together as part of the composition.

Giusti also created sculptural compositions for covers he created for *TV Guide* from the mid-1970s into the 1980s. In one of his most elaborate constructions for a publication, Giusti's cover for *TV Guide*'s January 20, 1979 Super Bowl XIII issue pictured his sculpture of a fully rounded head of a helmeted football player built from contrasting sheet metal, tubes, and plumbing fittings. Looking back in 1984, Giusti mused that if he had a chance to do them again, he would have executed some of his *Fortune* covers in three dimensions, "probably using Stainless Steel which is my favorite medium."[89]

Giusti, *Willy Brandt*, original art for the cover of *Time* (January 4, 1971). National Portrait Gallery, Smithsonian Institution; gift of *Time* magazine.

Giusti, cover for *TV Guide* (January 20–26, 1979). George Giusti Collection, Cary Graphic Arts Collection at The Wallace Center, Rochester Institute of Technology.

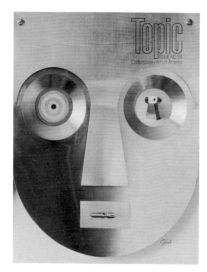

Giusti, cover for *Topic* no. 94 (1975).
George Giusti Collection,
Cary Graphic Arts Collection at
The Wallace Center,
Rochester Institute of Technology.

90 Morse, 26; also mentioned in Ball, 33;
Authors' interview with Robert Giusti,
August 27, 2014.

91 Giusti, "The Art Directors Club of
New York," 475.

In a series of the official commissions that echoed his work for the government in the 1940s, Giusti was able to bring his sculptural aesthetic to several projects. *America* was a Cold War propagandistic magazine published by the US government and sold in the USSR and other Communist bloc countries in exchange for the *Soviet Life* magazine sold in the United States, and *Topic* was published by the US Information Agency for distribution in Africa. In Giusti's cover for a 1975 issue of *Topic*, a metal face included insets that referred to a well-established icon of American art, Jasper Johns's targets; but Giusti also included an illustrator's pen nib and a photo of one of his own small-scale sculptures.

Sculpture for Its Own Sake

Reflecting his education as an artist and his early ambitions to be a painter, Giusti was interested in a vast array of artistic styles, media, and periods. In 1965, Giusti said his strongest early influences were Mies van der Rohe, Paul Klee, and Piet Mondrian, but his son recalled that his father's artistic interests were diverse, from Fra Angelico and Giotto to Giorgio de Chirico, Edward Hopper, Mark Rothko, and Roy Lichtenstein.[90] Just as he valued deeply the rigorous breadth of his own artistic training, Giusti felt strongly that design should be considered within a broader understanding of the arts. Reflecting in 1961 on his oft-repeated role as a judge for the New York Art Directors' exhibitions, Giusti was gladdened by what he saw as a "vast flux in approaches" in contemporary design, but he suggested that "a better-balanced jury could be achieved by including–along with art directors– such people of professional taste as painters, sculptors and architects. The results should prove most efficacious."[91]

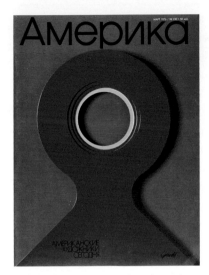

Giusti, cover for *America* (March 1976).
George Giusti Collection,
Cary Graphic Arts Collection at
The Wallace Center,
Rochester Institute of Technology.

92 Quoted in Bert, 22. A similar statement
    appears in "George Giusti," *Idea* 168
    (May 1980): 80.

93 Bert, 25–5; Authors' interview with
    Robert Giusti, August 27, 2014.

Giusti's desire to break down distinctions between design and art intensified as his career progressed, and he was determined to integrate the creative freedom associated with fine art with the conceptual rigor he demanded of design. In 1990, shortly after Giusti's death, Eileen Hedy Schultz, former president of the Art Directors Club and then creative director for Design International, recalled that Giusti "disdained the terms 'fine' and 'commercial art'… and believed that art is art, no matter what its purpose."[92] Indeed, Giusti transitioned fluidly between media and projects often associated with the commercial world and those sometimes seen as belonging to the realm of fine art, bringing from his work for design clients the same creative conceptualism applied in his own sculpture and architecture.

It is not terribly surprising that Giusti began to pursue sculpture for its own sake, freed from the requirements of its application to two-dimensional design projects. He had been creating three-dimensional constructions for graphic design projects since the early 1950s, and he created designs for three-dimensional Geigy packaging and for student supply kits for the Famous Artists School. He enjoyed working with tools, facilitating his design efficiency and his fastidious nature by constructing his own taboret and crafting masterful leather cases for his drafting tools, and his love of music and stringed instruments led him to restore antique lutes. Giusti was also a bit of a car enthusiast, babying a 1964 Porsche that he had purchased new, and tinkering with a Mark 10 Jaguar, for which he went so far as to fashion a new fender out of stainless steel rather than take it to a body shop for repair.[93]

94 George Giusti, quoted in *Variations on a Theme: Fifty Years of Graphic Arts in America*, ed. Will Burtin (Champion Papers, Inc., 1966), n.p. Invited to contribute to the 1966 AIGA exhibition "Variations on a Theme: Fifty Years of Graphic Arts in America," Giusti created a sculpture from metal and found images for which he cut holes in rectangular pieces of aluminum sheeting he purchased on Canal Street in New York (surprisingly for an artist of such precision, he reported that he managed to damage his parquet floor in the process). In contrast to the space age aluminum, he included a found image of a man who he initially thought would be a debonair face of the past, but was amused to find the face was actually from a police wanted poster for a criminal known as "Broken Nose George."

95 The subjects, chosen in a collaboration between Giusti and the magazine, were Edward Heath, Richard Nixon, Pope Paul, Mao Tse-tung, Golda Meir, Greta Garbo, and Mick Jagger. Ball, 28–33; 35.

When it came to creative work, given the chance, Giusti relished the opportunity to, as he put it in 1966, "create something just to my liking and no strings attached," to "work with a free mind and no worries about copy, typography and size." And given that freedom, he preferred to work in three dimensions.[94]

In 1971, Giusti was commissioned by London's *Daily Telegraph Magazine* to do a series of seven portrait sculptures in metal. All of the works reduced the subjects to salient, recognizable features, but he refrained from being cartoonish or creating caricatures. Giusti incorporated simplified forms and materials that could reflect the character of his subjects, and he explained his intentions: Golda Meir was crafted from weathered steel juxtaposed with more refined sheets of brass and tin, to refer to "the woman with a mind of steel"; elusive Greta Garbo's all-white face was rendered in a few simple elegant shapes, "beauty… translated into geometry"; Mick Jagger's face was a topography of planes painted in brash colors, "the devilish exponent of psychedelic pop music." Perhaps the most grandiose of the series was Giusti's Mao Tse-tung, whose torqued planar face emerged from a seven-foot-wide painted aluminum disc. Collaborating with an engineer friend, Giusti designed Mao's mechanized eyes so that they would impassively scan the room over and over.[95]

Giusti working on, "Mao Tse-tung,"
c. 1971–2, painted aluminum and
brass, mechanical elements,
diameter approximately 7.5 feet.
Photograph by Victor Keppler.
George Giusti Collection,
Cary Graphic Arts Collection
at The Wallace Center,
Rochester Institute of Technology.

Giusti, untitled sculpture, 1975,
stainless steel, 4 x 4 x 14 inches.
George Giusti Collection,
Cary Graphic Arts Collection
at The Wallace Center,
Rochester Institute of Technology.

96 "Advertising News," *New York Times*, November 23, 1944, 45; "National Club Opens Display of War Art," *New York Times*, December 22, 1944, 15; Morse, 28; Museum of Modern Art, "Emilio Ambasz and the Latin American Industrial Design Project," press release, April 25, 1970, 2; Joseph S. McLaughlin III and Virginia Mann Haggin McLaughlin, *Connecticut Painting, Drawing and Sculpture 78* (New Haven, CT: Art Resources of Connecticut, 1978).

Throughout his American career, Giusti's graphic design work had been exhibited extensively. In 1944, relatively soon after arriving in the United States, Giusti exhibited his advertising work at the A-D Gallery in New York in a joint exhibition with fellow European émigré and *Fortune*-cover designer Hans Moller. He would continue to exhibit internationally regularly, including a 1965 exhibition at Gallery 303, the reincarnation of the A-D Gallery, and in a 1967 traveling exhibition hosted by Princeton of "Geigy Graphics," which was designed by Emilio Ambasz, who would become curator of design at the Museum of Modern Art in 1968.

By the 1970s, Giusti was exhibiting his sculptures at fine art venues such as 1978's "Connecticut Painting, Drawing and Sculpture,"; and in the 1980s he was pursuing corporate and civic commissions for large-scale works.[96]

Giusti, column, c. early 1970s, installed at Giusti's West Redding House, stainless steel, approximately 10 feet high. Photograph from the Collection of Robert Giusti.

97 Authors' interview with Robert Giusti, August 28, 2015.

98 Authors' interview with Robert Giusti, August 27, 2014; "Gilbert C. Tompkins, a Historian of Golf and Art Representative, 94," *New York Times*, August 23, 1977, 37; "Tour of Homes on Long Island to Aid Hospital: Saturday Event Slated for Proposed South Shore Institution," *New York Times*, May 11, 1960, 35.

Giusti's sculpture completed for its own sake (rather than as a component of a graphic design project) tended toward abstraction, and he was especially fond of working in stainless steel. He favored geometric volumes such as cubes, pyramids, cones, and cylinders, and at times he included additional elements that made figurative references, as in his untitled work from 1975 with its eye-like projecting cylinders. Giusti often played with positive and negative spaces, piercing the masses of the sculptures with voids and recessed inner spaces and volumes. The scale in which Giusti worked varied widely, from diminutive sculptures just a few inches high to monumental works nearly 16 feet tall. Giusti designed the structure of the larger works with the help of engineer friend Larry Hough and partnered with Lippincott, Inc. to have them fabricated.[97] He installed one of his largest works, *Column No. 1*, in the yard of his Connecticut home. The massive stainless steel edifice was a play on solid and void, mass and airiness, with segmented cylindrical forms stacked and cut out in organic curves to reveal interior cavities and structures.

Attuned to Architectural Design

Beyond his work in design, painting, and sculpture, Giusti also pursued projects in interior design and architecture. Having cited Mies van der Rohe as an early influence and explained that his education at the Brera Academy included the study of architecture, Giusti seems to have been attuned to the design of three-dimensional spaces. Gilbert Tompkins, Giusti's first agent in the 1940s, was educated as an artist and also appreciated modern architecture, living in a 1945 Marcel Breuer-designed house on Lake Drive in Hewlitt Harbor, Long Island, that Giusti must have been familiar with and seems to have been inspired by.[98]

Giusti, Mendham House, interior,
mid-1960s. Photograph from
the Collection of Robert Giusti.

In his own architectural design, Giusti revealed a desire to
integrate spare modernist features with natural materials
and playful, sometimes quirky objects and artifacts, as Breuer
had done with Tompkins's home.

99 Johnson, 50, 80–1. During this period,
   Giusti had an apartment
   in New York City at 342 East 53rd Street.

100 Giusti, "Chiesa Vecchia,"
   typewritten manuscript, n.d.
   Collection of Robert Giusti.

Giusti remodeled the family summer home on Hilltop Road in Mendham, New Jersey, transforming an old colonial coach house on a large lot, into what Fridolf Johnson called in 1964 "a contemporary 'living machine' without... that contrived look that spoils so many 'modern' houses." As he considered Giusti's interior, Johnson continued,

> One had the feeling that in this house living and creation were interchangeable terms.... Everywhere were engaging witnesses of Giusti's fancy and ingenuity; unusual collector's items, furniture that he had built or done over and decorated; walls, beams, doorways, all bore the marks of his attention. In one corner of the room, easy chairs and sofas clustered around a coffee table made of a huge slab of rough stone. Suspended from the ceiling and almost touching the floor, was a bare tree about nine feet high. In its branches were a couple of tiny exquisitely carved birds. It was a charming conceit, and it seemed exactly right as a foil to the ponderous table."

And of course, Johnson pointed out, Giusti would need a workspace: "One long, narrow room had been converted into a bar. At one end was an immaculate carpenter's bench; above it hung, in ingenious home-made racks, an assortment of well-kept tools."[99]

Giusti, Chiesa Vecchia, exterior, mid-1960s.
Photograph from the
George Giusti Collection,
Cary Graphic Arts Collection
at The Wallace Center,
Rochester Institute of Technology.

Giusti, Chiesa Vecchia, interior, mid-1960s.
Photograph from the
George Giusti Collection,
Cary Graphic Arts Collection
at The Wallace Center,
Rochester Institute of Technology.

Another of Giusti's transformational remodeling projects was Chiesa Vecchia, a small former church with a twelfth-century tower in Prunarolo di Vergato, Italy, about 20 miles from Bologna, which he purchased as he spent more time in Europe working with Geigy. He combined the rustic stone shell of the church and tower with simple, functional, modernist elements, transforming the former sacristy of the church into a three-bedroom home with a soaring two-story living area. Giusti juxtaposed the exposed granite walls and twelfth-century fireplace with locally crafted modern construction such as a cantilevered chestnut staircase and balcony, Carrara marble floors, and custom furniture he himself designed, along with Le Corbusier chairs and monumental Noguchi lamps. The 1.5 acres of surrounding rural property included orchards and vineyards.[100]

Giusti, Sketch for Pomarico House,
c. mid-1960s.
Collection of Robert Giusti.

Giusti, Suter House, 1964, exterior.
Photograph from the
Collection of Robert Giusti.

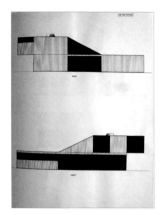

101 Giusti is also said to have designed a house for a dentist, Dr. Pomarico, in Connecticut. Authors' interview with Robert Giusti, August 27, 2014.

102 Pam Stebbins, "Meadowtop Garden: Fertile Ground for More than Flowers," *New Marlborough 5 Village News*, July 2002, 5; "100 acres sold for $75,000," *Berkshire Eagle*, October 19, 1972, 28; "145 Acres Offered to Land Trust," *Berkshire Eagle*, June 1, 1977, 31; Authors' interview with Arthur Fefferman, August 18, 2015. Special thanks to Joseph Poindexter and Alan Lombardi for help in pinpointing the Suter house.

Beyond remodeling existing architectural spaces, Giusti also designed several houses from scratch. He was commissioned to design houses for friends and colleagues, including a 1964 home for Geigy USA head Carl (Charles) Suter and his wife, Margrit, on their property in Mill River, Massachusetts.[101] The Suters, whose Crystal Hill Farm would ultimately grow to 600 acres through opportune land purchases, had first explored having a home built by one of several major modernist architects, but ultimately decided to enlist Giusti to design their house. Avid gardeners and land preservationists, the Suters had Giusti design a low, rectangular house high on a hillside overlooking the rolling hills of southern Massachusetts and northern Connecticut.[102] Working with architect Crane De Camp, Giusti integrated a variety of natural materials that linked the house to the pastures and woods that surrounded it. Flagstone floors on the porch, terrace, and entryway linked interior and exterior spaces with roofed outside spaces that acted as intermediaries between the living areas and the outside. On the south side, the plane of the low-pitched roof extended beyond the wall with an overhang open to the sky. The approach to the front door on the north revealed sets of glass doors that allowed one to see through the house to the panoramic views to the south. A wide flagstone hearth and chimney created a core to the public areas of the house, the centerpiece of an open plan between the dining and living areas. Giusti continued the focus on natural materials with oak floors, wooden cabinetry with custom-designed mahogany pulls, and wooden exterior siding, and he used fieldstone in the retaining walls for the terraced slope of the yard and gardens around the house.

103 Giusti's son Robert reported that the West Redding house was engineered with the help of a member of the Breuer studio. Giusti listed himself as the designer, and the architect as Crane De Camp of Pound Ridge, New York, his collaborator on the Suter house as well. Authors' interview with Robert Giusti, August 27, 2014; Giusti, "Designer's Statement," typewritten manuscript, c. 1969, George Giusti Collection, Cary Graphic Arts Collection at The Wallace Center, Rochester Institute of Technology.

104 Giusti, "Owner-Designer-Statement," typewritten manuscript, c. 1969, n.p. [one year after completion of the house], George Giusti Collection, Cary Graphic Arts Collection at The Wallace Center, Rochester Institute of Technology.

105 Giusti, "Designer's Statement," n.p.

Giusti's most noteworthy architectural project was a home he designed for himself and his wife around 1968 on ten acres of land in West Redding, Connecticut, outside of Danbury.[103] The house, along with a studio and garage building, were fabricated out of more modern, industrial materials than the house he had designed for the Suters, including Mayari-R weathering structural steel, a material that would form a protective layer of rust when left open to the elements. In his owner-designer statement, Giusti explained that "the austerity of the silhouette and the clarity of its lines lend to the buildings a timeless, classical character." He wrote, "When I first started to lay down the groundwork of my future home, it was with the hope to create a functional, contemporary structure which would reflect my personal taste and show distinctly the essence of my philosophy as an artist and a designer.... It had to be practical, easy to run, stripped of any complicated detail and void of any superficial embellishments. It was not to be a 'decorator's' house. I figured, that by abiding strictly to this principle, the result would not only be crystal clear in concept, but also beautiful." While a few walls were clad in steel, many were large, bronze-tinted sheets of plate glass, a combination of materials Giusti felt was "not at all cold and mechanical in feeling. On the contrary; the beautiful deep color of the weathering steel and the bronze tint of the glass walls are warm and human."[104] In the interior, Giusti contrasted the industrial materials of the structure with understated natural materials: slate tiled floors, ebony counters and cabinets, and travertine stair treads.[105] Giusti's studio was attached to the garage of the house—not surprisingly, it was meticulously organized with the perfectionism he extended to every project, no matter how small.

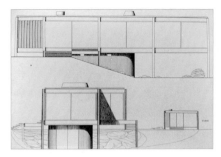

Giusti, West Redding House, elevations, c. 1968. Photograph from the Collection of Robert Giusti.

Giusti, West Redding House, exterior, c. 1968. Photograph from the Collection of Robert Giusti.

In 1972, Ian Ball, a writer for the British *Daily Telegraph Magazine*, marveled at Giusti's West Redding home:

> Surely nowhere is there an artist's studio like this. It might be the reception room of some dazzlingly modern headquarters designed for a computer company. Two of the walls are of sheer glass, the lighting and access to a charming view of rolling Connecticut countryside being controlled by white vertical louvers. One has become accustomed to the clutter and disarray of artists' workspaces. Here there is a precise place for everything and an awesome sense of order. There is not the merest nick or paint splatter on the white walls and white desk.

106 Ball, 35.

107 "George Giusti," *Idea*, 80;
  "Art Directors Club Hall of Fame:
  George Giusti," 128. Giusti was
  in good company–his fellow 1979
  Art Directors Club Hall of Fame inductees
  included Milton Glaser, W. A. Dwiggins,
  Ladislav Sutnar, and Jan Tschichold.
  Philip H. Dougherty, "Advertising:
  Art Directors Honored," *New York Times*,
  October 24, 1979, 17.

In his studio as in his home, every item of furniture or equipment is a modern classic, a painstaking tribute to Bauhaus taste in the refinement of design. The art is an eclectic mixture of modern paintings by his friends or by members of his own family. Occasionally, as a counterpoint touch, a carefully chosen antique–a collection of 17th-century Italian stringed instruments, or a superb model of a 19th-century steam engine–is positioned on the white walls.[106]

As he had hoped, Giusti had created a home that reflected his design sense. It was functional, modern, and pared down to the essential, but retained meaningful references that communicated effectively, in this case, who he was as a designer and an artist.

Honors and Accolades

In 1979, upon being inducted into the Art Directors Hall of Fame, Giusti was said to have "avoided the classical and sought instead a contemporary, even futuristic effect. He has succeeded to the extent that his designs are consistently ahead of their time."[107] Throughout his career, Giusti evolved as a designer; yet he consistently maintained a balance between the cerebral, abstract language of modernism and meaningful, apprehensible symbolism. He displayed the remarkable ability to maneuver in a field that shifted significantly as he practiced for more than half a century, excelling both in a midcentury era when fortunate progressive designers were given a great deal of creative latitude by adventuresome clients, and in later decades when corporate clients tended to demand more input.

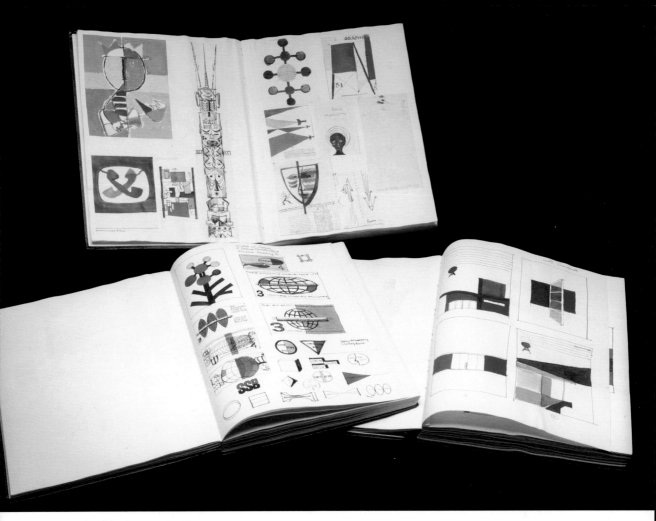

Giusti sketchbooks, c. 1950s–70s,
George Giusti Collection,
Cary Graphic Arts Collection
at The Wallace Center,
Rochester Institute of Technology.

108 Johnson, 82.

In addition to his Hall of Fame induction, Giusti earned score upon score of medals, awards, and citations for his design work; yet perhaps the most telling testimony to his career is the work he left behind when he died in 1990.

The depth and scope of his oeuvre that is preserved in the George Giusti Collection at the Rochester Institute of Technology, is an awe-inspiring manifestation of his design philosophy, his lifelong assertion, as Fridolf Johnson relayed it, that "good design is not a matter of whim, or of adapting the tricks of others, but the product of logical thinking and honest craftsmanship."[108]

ACKNOWLEDGMENTS

The authors would like to thank our collaborators at RIT, Kari Horowicz and Molly Q. Cort; Robert and Grace Giusti for their hospitality and generosity in giving us access to their archives; Jayson Dobney for sharing his expertise on musical instruments; Dick Whitney for helping to date some of Giusti's early work; Joseph Poindexter, Alan Lombardi, and Arthur Fefferman for helping us pinpoint the location of Giusti's Suter house; Joan Cummins for her judicious editing; and Drew McManus and Grace Sternberger for their patience.

ABOUT THE AUTHORS

Ned Drew

Professor Ned Drew heads the Graphic Design area at Rutgers University-Newark, where he teaches various design and design history courses. Drew is a member of the AIGA National Design Educators Community Steering Committee and the Director of The Design Consortium, a student/teacher-run design studio that focuses on nonprofit, community-based projects.

Drew is the co-editor of *Design Education in Progress: Process and Methodology, Volumes 1, 2,* and *3,* and co-author (with Paul Sternberger) of *By Its Cover: Modern American Book Cover Design* (2005) and *Purity of Aim: The Book Jacket Designs of Alvin Lustig* (2010).

Drew is also a founding partner of the multidisciplinary design firm BRED, which is based in New York City (www.brednation.com). His work has been included in the sixth edition of *Typographic Design: Form and Communication, Graphic Design Referenced, US Design 1975–2000, Working with Computer Type,* the AIGA's *Rethinking Design 3: Speaking Volumes, Graphic Design Solutions, Color Management for Logos* and 2D: *Visual Basics for Designers* and has been recognized by the AIGA, The Type Directors Club, the International Design Awards, the Art Directors Club, Creativity, the FPO Awards, the UCDA and the AAM as well as *Graphis, Communication Arts, Print,* and *How* magazines.

Brenda McManus

Brenda McManus is an Assistant Professor of Graphic Design at Pace University and founding partner and creative director of the multidisciplinary design firm BRED (www.brednation.com). Her work focuses on the creation of expressive, functional typography and typographic systems. Her work has appeared in *Graphic Design Solutions*, *Color Management for Logos*, and *Color Management: A Comprehensive Guide for Graphic Designers*, and her student work has appeared in the most recent edition of *Typographic Design: Form and Communication*. McManus has been recognized by several design publications, including *Print*, *Graphis* and *How* magazines, and by organizations such as the Art Directors Club, the Type Directors Club, the University & College Designers Association, the Museum Publications Design Competition, and the Creativity Design Competition. Her work has been included in the TDC46 Awards Exhibition, Summit–an AIGA/NY Exhibition, the 37th ADCNJ Awards Show, the UCDA Conference Exhibition and the American Association of Museum Design Exhibition.

Paul Sternberger

Paul Sternberger, Associate Professor of Art History at Rutgers University-Newark, specializes in American Art and the History of Photography. His publications include *Between Amateur and Aesthete: The Legitimization of Photography in America, 1880–1900* and *India: Public Places, Private Spaces–Contemporary Photography and Video Art*. Sternberger's articles and reviews have appeared in journals such as *American Art*, *Photographies*, the *Journal of the History of Collections*, and *The Woman's Art Journal*. Collaborating with Rutgers-Newark colleague Ned Drew, he published *By Its Cover: Modern American Book Cover Design* and *Purity of Aim: The Book Jackets of Alvin Lustig*.

COLOPHON

Design	Bruce Ian Meader
Editor	Molly Q. Cort
Production	Marnie Soom
Typefaces	Sabon designed by Jan Tschichold and Frutiger designed by Adrian Frutiger
Paper	Cover: 14 point ProductoLith Text: 80 pound Huron Gloss
Printing	Thomson-Shore Dexter, Michigan